25 PATTERNS TO
HAUNT YOUR HOME

Witchy stitching

MEG BLACK

Creator of The Witchy Stitcher

HERBERT PRESS
LONDON · OXFORD · NEW YORK · NEW DELHI · SYDNEY

HERBERT PRESS
Bloomsbury Publishing Plc
50 Bedford Square, London, WC1B 3DP, UK
Bloomsbury Publishing Ireland Limited
29 Earlsfort Terrace, Dublin 2, D02 AY28, Ireland

BLOOMSBURY, HERBERT PRESS and the Herbert Press logo are
trademarks of Bloomsbury Publishing Plc

First published in Great Britain in 2025

Copyright © Meg Black, 2025

Meg Black has asserted her right under the
Copyright, Designs and Patents Act, 1988, to be
identified as Author of this work

All rights reserved. No part of this publication may be: i) reproduced or transmitted in any form, electronic or mechanical, including photocopying, recording or by means of any information storage or retrieval system without prior permission in writing from the publishers; or ii) used or reproduced in any way for the training, development or operation of artificial intelligence (AI) technologies, including generative AI technologies. The rights holders expressly reserve this publication from the text and data mining exception as per Article 4(3) of the Digital Single Market Directive (EU) 2019/790

Bloomsbury Publishing Plc does not have any control over, or responsibility for, any third-party websites referred to or in this book. All internet addresses given in this book were correct at the time of going to press. The author and publisher regret any inconvenience caused if addresses have changed or sites have ceased to exist, but can accept no responsibility for any such changes

A catalogue record for this book is available from the British Library
Library of Congress Cataloguing-in-Publication data has been applied for

ISBN: 978-1-7899-4224-8; eBook: 978-1-7899-4225-5

4 6 8 10 9 7 5

Various graphics and icons © 4zevar/Adobe Stock; nadzeya26/Adobe Stock; Olga/Adobe Stock; artvea/Getty Images; Alesikka/iStock; MariaTkach/iStock; Sudowoodo/iStock; AS Prinon/Shutterstock; dja-karta/Shutterstock; In Art/Shutterstock; Leena Uskova/Shutterstock; VectorPot/Shutterstock

Pattern-themed ghost illustrations © Alex Black

Typeset in Dovetail MVB
Designed by Austin Taylor
Printed and bound in Italy by L.E.G.O. S.p.A.

To find out more about our authors and books visit www.bloomsbury.com and sign up for our newsletters
For product safety related questions contact productsafety@bloomsbury.com

Contents

Introduction 4
About the author 6

Macabre materials 8
The Witchy Stitcher's guide to stitchcraft 20
Bookmark tutorial 37
Being 'extra': beads, antiquing, dyeing fabric and customizing! 42
Stitching vernacular 52

Patterns 54

For the coven: witchy patterns with a touch of darkness 56

Gothic gallery: haunted creations with a dash of whimsy 86

Halloween: pumpkins, ghosts and bats – oh my! 118

Haunted holidays: holiday-inspired patterns with a creepy twist 158

Finishing tips and tricks 182

Acknowledgments 189
Suppliers 190

Introduction

Welcome to the haunted corner of cross stitch. Inside this stitchcraft grimoire you will find 25 patterns (plus two bonus designs) with which to bewitch your home. Cross stitch is an art form that has been around longer than the ghost in your attic. Traces of the craft have been found on cloth fragments dating all the way back to the sixth century! A modern resurgence has created space for niche artists like me to let their creep flags fly. The stitching community is unlike any I have ever participated in – it truly is 'finding your people'. If you are new to the craft, I highly recommend finding like-minded stitchers and sharing your work! Folks are quick to compliment and encourage fellow fabric stabbers.

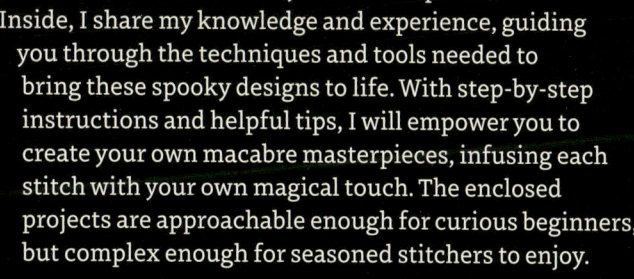

Within the pages of this grimoire, I unveil a collection of haunting and unique patterns that will transport you to a realm where shadows dance and magic lingers in the air. Each pattern is a glimpse into my mind: a world of magic and things that go bump in the night.

The book before you is more than a mere collection of patterns: it is a guided tour into a world of creativity and self-expression.

Inside, I share my knowledge and experience, guiding you through the techniques and tools needed to bring these spooky designs to life. With step-by-step instructions and helpful tips, I will empower you to create your own macabre masterpieces, infusing each stitch with your own magical touch. The enclosed projects are approachable enough for curious beginners, but complex enough for seasoned stitchers to enjoy.

So, gather your threads, sharpen your needles, and prepare to embark on a journey into witchy stitching. It is time to unleash the magic in your fingertips!

About the author

Even as a young witchling I was crafty, creative, fascinated and enamored by the darker side of things. I truly embody the Halloween lifestyle in my everyday life and through my work. It really is Halloween every day at the Witchy Haunt.

Throughout many career changes, I always had a little artsy business on the side. I began my education by obtaining a Bachelor of Fine Arts (BFA) degree, which led me down a path of strange graphic design jobs where I found myself emptying garbage and acquiring the dark ichor of the gods for my masters. I wasn't happy, or artistically fulfilled. I wound up in nursing school where I became a Licensed Practical Nurse. At this point I had a child to take care of and knew I needed something stable so that I could raise my delightful spawn. Between and during my art and nursing careers I frequently went back to my reliable bartending skills. In the background, I was pushing my art constantly in a variety of media, from fine arts, clothing, sculpture, and eventually to fiber craft. It was always my dream to have a creative job, but one that gave me the freedom to forge my own path. Eventually, I retired from nursing and returned to management and bartending, where I fell into running a music venue. It was at this time of my life that The Witchy Stitcher was born.

It was a crisp Canadian winter, the December of 2017, and funds were low, so my family and I decided to have a handmade holiday. While scrolling through online image boards, I stumbled across cute and kitschy cross stitch patterns, and thought, 'I am sure I could make everyone a custom cross stitch'. I hadn't stitched since I was a kid, but I still knew the basics pretty well and had a little training in pixel art. Fast forward to New Year's Eve, and I posted a pattern to an online marketplace. Within an hour I heard the little 'cha-ching!' of a sale. I shot out of bed and did a little happy dance – the fire was lit. For the next six months I continued managing the music venue and working on The Witchy Stitcher. By the summer of 2018, I knew I had something tangible and decided to nurture my little dark stitch baby full time. Filled with passion and drive, I had found my home: and somewhere I could truly be myself and create my own world.

For the first three years, I didn't take a day off; I am not even kidding. My shop began to overflow with patterns, handmade kits, unique cross stitch accessories and mystery boxes. It was beginning to overwhelm me, and I admit that I worked myself into a nervous breakdown. I pushed myself too hard for too long, and the stress of keeping up appearances and expectations wore me down. After a month-long break, I came back refreshed and with a new plan to continue growing the business while keeping my sanity. I learned to say 'no', take days off, enjoy the ride and be gentler with my body and mind. This is when the magic bloomed, and The Witchy Stitcher became what it is today. I have a healthy work-life balance and feel that the quality of my work has improved as a result.

One of my dreams has always been to publish an art book; it was something I thought about often. So, when I was approached by Bloomsbury Publishing it is safe to say I leaped at the chance. I immediately got to work planning patterns and content. With only a few months to go before the deadline, I was diagnosed with a rare blood cancer. Was I scared of cancer? Of course, but I was also scared of losing the book, my footing with The Witchy Stitcher and the beautiful connections I had made with people all over the world. I was hesitant to make my health concerns public but, ultimately, I did. The outpouring of love and support blew my mind. I couldn't believe that within an instant, I had an army of people showering with me with support and holding me up. I didn't lose a thing. Instead, I gained companionship and a level of connection I didn't think possible. I know many of you are reading this right now, and I just want to say from the bottom of my heart, thank you.

Fast forward to a year later and I am sitting here writing these words, the cancer is stable, and I am feeling more like my old self again. I don't know if things will ever be as they were before, but I am embracing my new normal and my changed perspective on life. If I have learned anything over this past year it is to not sweat the small stuff, and big, scary mountains can be conquered. Most important of all, give yourself as many moments of joy as possible.

Why cross stitch is good for your mental health

Cross stitch is a meditative craft that, speaking personally, has done wonders for my anxiety, stress and depression. Stitching requires you to be present in the moment and concentrate fully on the task at hand. This often clears the mind of stress or worries, creating a calmer state of mind. Silence is very hard to achieve in our information-saturated digital world. Who knew that cross stitch was so closely related to mindfulness? You might not discover this soothing dimension while you are beginning to learn the craft but, trust me, it will come. Once you become more familiar with the physical process, it just happens. The icing on the mental health cake is that while you are calming your mind, you are creating a work of art that you can be proud of.

Meg Black
THE WITCHY STITCHER

Macabre materials

Behind every successful cross stitch project lies a trove of materials essential to the craft. Not sure what the bits and bobs and the fancy stitching tools are? Need a refresher? In this grimoire entry we will go over the basic stitchcraft accessories, from fabric types and choosing the right needle, to organizing your projects and all the voids between.

MACABRE MATERIALS

Fabric

Three different types of fabric are commonly used for cross stitch: aida, evenweave and linen. They come in a wide variety of counts (ct) and colors. The number of squares per inch correlates to the fabric count, e.g.:

- **14CT AIDA:** 14 squares per inch = 14 stitches per inch
- **30CT LINEN:** 30 squares per inch = 30 stitches per inch

The fabric count directly relates to the finished size of your work of art and will vary depending on what count you use. We will cover that in more depth on pages 22–23.

Whether it's aida, with its visible grid pattern, or evenweave and linen, with their delicate, elegant textures, each fabric offers a unique canvas for stitching. They come in a rainbow of colors too, from plain to wild and wonderful explosions of color. Larger fabric brands offer a wide range of options, but indie fabric dyers are where the magic really lies. Throughout this grimoire, I have used fabrics from many small businesses, some hand-dyed, others printed … it's all here!

Choosing your fabric can seem overwhelming, and with so many to select from, getting started can feel like opening a closet full of monsters. But knowledge is power – grab your shovel … we're about to dig in.

Aida

Aida was created specifically for cross stitch in the late 1800s by the German company Zweigart. They remain the largest manufacturer of aida, and I am not one to play favorites, but it is my preferred brand. Their fabric is smooth as butter and a dream to stitch on. It is a cotton fabric with a grid made up of visible holes, which makes it easy for beginners to use as the grid guides the placement of stitches in a pattern. Even seasoned stitchers prefer it, as it is straightforward to use, affordable and available in most craft and big-box stores.

Common aida counts are 11, 14, 16, 18 and 22, with the most popular being 14ct.

Evenweave

Evenweave fabric has a grid layout where the threads in both directions are evenly spaced, hence the name evenweave. Typically, they are a mix of natural (cotton) and synthetic (rayon) threads. Evenweave is slightly less stiff than aida but sturdier than linen, and it is not as widely available as either aida or linen.

Evenweave comes in a variety of counts, most commonly 25, 28, 30 and 32.

GHOST TIP

If you are just embarking on your magical stitching journey, I recommend starting with 14ct aida. Try a lighter-colored fabric first, as the darker the fabric, the more difficult it is to stitch on. When using darker fabrics, a little trick is to place something light on your lap or behind your project. This makes the holes more visible!

ABOVE Here is what the same project looks like on 14ct aida (right) and 28ct linen (left). The pattern for this ghostly piece is on page 24.

Linen

Linen is the choice of many experienced stitchers because of its soft touch and higher thread counts. Because linen is woven from natural flax fibers, not all threads will have the same thickness, therefore making it not completely even, and the stitches per inch may not be the same count vertically as horizontally. The linen fibers also have natural imperfections that show up as 'slubs'. These are not defects, but a hallmark of this beautiful, natural material. Personally, I love the irregular, organic look of linen. It creates an aesthetically aged appearance that makes my black heart beat a little faster. Linen is more expensive than cotton fabrics like aida but is nearly as easy to obtain.

Linen comes in the largest selection of counts, most commonly 18, 22, 26, 28, 30, 32, 35, 40, 36 and 50.

FUN WITCHY STITCHER FACT
I only learned how to stitch on linen a few years ago. My whole stitching career before that I used aida. I prefer linen now, but I enjoy going back to aida for certain projects, especially if I am working on a black background (although I do enjoy tormenting myself with high-count black linens from time to time – they just look so beautiful!).

~ MACABRE MATERIALS ~

Thread

The main thread used for cross stitch is stranded cotton, also known as embroidery thread or floss. Stranded cotton is made up of six divisible strands of loosely twisted thread. For cross stitch you usually only need to use two or three of these strands. It is often sold in skeins, about 315 inches (8 meters) long. As you only use a few strands of thread at a time, a skein can go a long way – you can usually make 1,700–2,000 stitches when using two strands together. This varies depending on how thrifty a stitcher you are and how scattered the colors are within the pattern.

There are many different manufacturers and artisans of embroidery thread. For my patterns, I use DMC embroidery thread, so we will focus on them. DMC, short for 'Dollfus-Mieg & Compagnie', has a rich heritage of quality and innovation in the world of fiber arts. DMC thread has been made in the same factory in Mulhouse, France since its inception in 1898. I choose to use this brand as it is the most accessible worldwide and has very consistent quality in both the thread itself as well as the colors.

> **GRIMOIRE FACT**
> If you stitch all the projects in this grimoire you will have used 30 skeins of DMC 310.

DMC Stranded Cotton

This is easily the most widely used thread in cross stitch, and it comes in a cosmic color range of over 500 shades! Possessing a full DMC floss library is many a stitcher's dream, and a milestone when reached. All my designs use DMC Stranded Cotton as the main thread.

DMC Light Effects

Light Effects are mostly metallic, but the range also includes some neon threads and the popular Glow in the Dark (GITD) option. These threads can be a bit tricky to work with, but the results are well worth the extra effort. Some may disagree – these threads are also nicknamed 'The Devil's Hair' for their nightmarish qualities, and many stitchers avoid them like the plague.

Each metallic Light Effects color has a matching Stranded Cotton. You can match them by adding an E to the Stranded Cotton number. For example, 310 is my beloved black Stranded Cotton, and E310 is black, but with a slight shine to it.

You will find the Glow in the Dark (E940) Light Effects thread used throughout this grimoire.

DMC Étoile

These are cotton threads with some added glitter. Étoile (French for 'star') flosses have a beautiful yet subtle sparkle. They are much easier to stitch with compared to Light Effects threads.

Each glittering shade has a matching Stranded Cotton, and, as with Light Effects, you can match them by adding a C to the Stranded Cotton number. For example, C310 is black, but with sparkles running through it.

You will find this shimmering floss used throughout this grimoire.

ABOVE Glow in the Dark thread showcased on page 172.

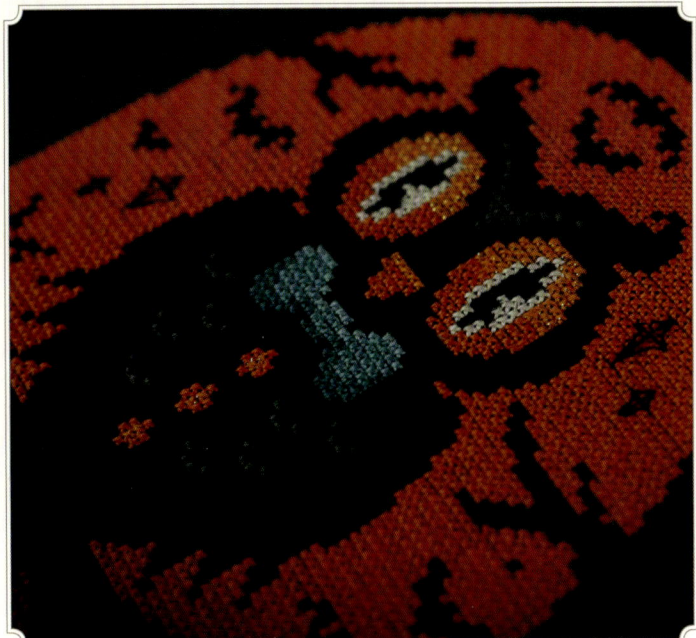

LEFT The subtle orange sparkle in this owl's eyes is DMC Étoile.

with and give a unique result every time. When using these threads, you want to ensure you make the individual cross stitches one at a time to maximize that variegated effect.

Hand-dyed thread

Just when you thought the thread world was gigantic already, hand-dyed thread artists materialize! Hand-dyed thread, like hand-dyed fabric, is available in a monstrous rainbow of options from indie artists and large established businesses.

Hand-dyed thread fills the voids in the DMC color library and offers beautiful, variegated options. When you stitch with them, the color patterns are always unique, while DMC Variegated threads are predictable. Hand-dyed threads add a little bit of extra interest to your work and are great for filling large areas to create depth and interest.

Although I adore hand-dyed threads, I don't use them often in my designs for a few reasons. They can be quite costly and are harder to obtain because stock is not guaranteed. Dye lots can vary, resulting in inconsistent color and intensity. This can work to your advantage, because you will always produce something truly unique, but it is unlikely that you will achieve the same look twice.

I do, however, always urge anyone who stitches my designs to use hand-dyed thread. It is great fun to work with, and a perfect way to add your own magical touch to your creation. I love to use it in my personal projects and for special collaborations.

DMC Satin

Satin threads are the shiniest of the bunch and are made of 100 per cent rayon. I find them the hardest to work with, but they do yield beautiful results. I prefer to use them for embroidery rather than cross stitch.

As before, each Satin shade has a matching Stranded Cotton. This time, the letter used is S, so S310 is black, but with a lustrous sheen.

DMC Variegated and Variations

Variations and Variegated threads are similar in that they feature multiple colors throughout the same skein. Variegated threads use different tones of the same color, while Variations use multiple complementary colors.

These threads do not have DMC Stranded Cotton equivalents because of the multiple tones or colors used in each. However, you can find solid DMC colors that will match one or multiple shades used in the skein.

Variegated and Variations often have high-contrast color changes, going from super dark to super light. They are a lot of fun to work

Needles

Cross stitch is usually worked with a tapestry needle; its blunt tip can easily pass through your specialty cross stitch fabric without splitting the fibers. A sharper needle, such as an embroidery or sewing needle, is harder to control, and you might find yourself coming up through a different place in your fabric than you intended, or splitting your stitches and making them look messy. The horror!

The most commonly used tapestry needle sizes for cross stitch are size 24 and 26, however they are available in sizes 18, 20, 22, 24, 26 and 28. My needle of choice is size 26 for almost the entirety of my stitching. The strange thing with needle sizing is the lower the number the bigger the needle – makes perfect sense, right?

RIGHT Use this diagram to help you choose your needle size.

A sharp-tipped needle is useful for backstitch or beadwork, and many stitchers gravitate toward specialty needles for these techniques. Embroidery needles work well

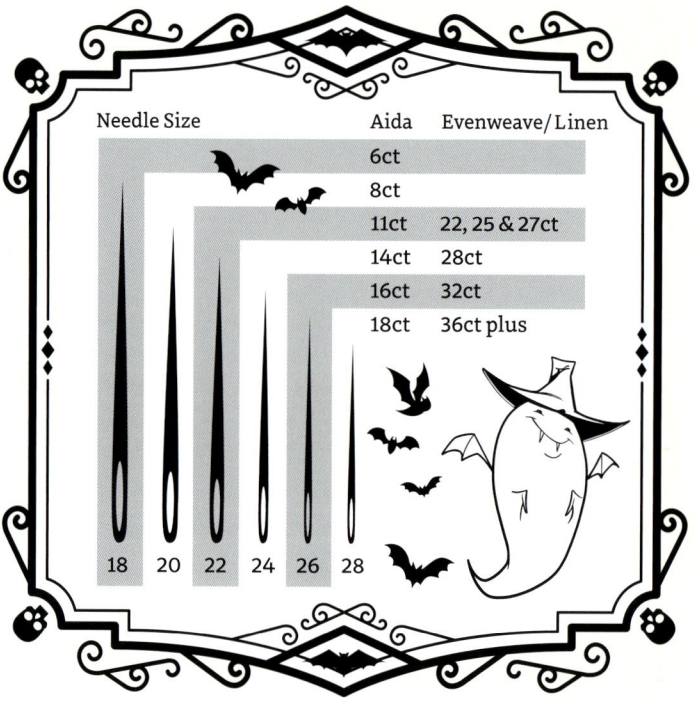

Needle Size	Aida	Evenweave/Linen
	6ct	
	8ct	
	11ct	22, 25 & 27ct
	14ct	28ct
	16ct	32ct
	18ct	36ct plus

18 20 22 24 26 28

for backstitching because they have sharp tips, can be easier to control and place cleaner backstitches. Bead needles obviously are great for – you guessed it – beads!

Needle minders

Let us set the scene … there you are, all cozied up with a good movie, stitching into the night. You get up to replenish your snacks, only to return to a mischievously absconding needle! You panic, and search the blankets, the floor, your clothes… You have visions of it going into your foot or, even worse, one of your fur babies getting hold of it! This is where the magical needle minder is your savior.

A needle minder (or needle nanny) is a magnetic tool that attaches to your project, giving you a safe place to pop your needle when not in use. These magnificent accessories are made up of a decorative front piece glued to a magnet, and a second removable magnet. Simply sandwich your project between the magnets, and that's it!

The most exciting part about needle minders is the vast selection available to purchase; there is a whole wacky, spooky and cute assortment out there. Of course, you can always make your own. In my experience, the best magnets to use are neodymium rare earth magnets.

GHOST TIP
Be sure to test the magnetic strength of your needle minder before you make it. Some materials can weaken the magnetism, and your needle may not stick securely to the minder.

Scissors

Cross stitch is delicate work that often has you working in tight spaces, so small sewing scissors are the prime choice for this craft. Compact scissors allow you to snip safely and accurately at the back of your project.

I recommend having a dedicated pair of scissors (or ten) in your cross stitch accessory hoard. Using them only to snip your threads keeps them as sharp as your wit and will ensure them a long, healthy life. I am sure you have heard the scary tales of fabric or sewing scissors being used to cut (gasp) paper! Using your fancy snips to cut things other than your thread can quickly dull them, resulting in frayed thread ends.

My scissors of choice are pointed beauties no longer than 4-6in (10-15cm).

Hoops and frames

There are lots of different ways to hold your project. Whether you use a frame or not is up to you. Beginner stitchers may find it easier to put their fabric in an embroidery hoop or frame. Another option is to stitch in hand without the use of hoops or frames.

Hoops and frames come in a variety of sizes to suit your needs and preferences. I like to use a frame that doesn't require that I move it often to continue stitching. For example, if I am making a project where the stitched area is 5 x 8in (13 x 20cm) I will opt to use either a 9in (22cm) hoop or an 8 x 10in (20 x 25.5cm) snap frame. Both will allow the entire stitched area to sit within the frame and I won't have to move it during stitching.

Hoop and frame options

★ **EMBROIDERY HOOPS:** the classic go-to for cross stitch and embroidery. They comprise two hoops that fit snugly together with a screw at the top to control the tension.
★ **SNAP FRAMES:** rectangular plastic frames that have C-shaped plastic clamps to hold your fabric taut.
★ **SPRING TENSION HOOPS:** similar to embroidery hoops, but instead of the screw apparatus, the tension is created using a flexible inner hoop that springs open to hold the fabric in place.
★ **SCROLL FRAMES:** great for extra-large projects. They comprise a frame with two rolling bars to which you sew or staple your fabric.

Excess fabric woes

Some lesser-known stitching accessories are tools to hold your excess fabric while it is on your hoop or frame. When sewing larger projects, there may be lots of fabric that can get in the way and slow down your stitching.

My favorite is the grime guard; they are fangtastic for holding unruly fabric and keeping your project clean from snack-dusted fingertips, hence the name. These fabric and elastic creations look exactly like a steering wheel cover (which can also work!). You can make your own if you are sew-savvy, or they are available from a plethora of online retailers both big and small. I prefer to get custom guards in spooky fabric designs.

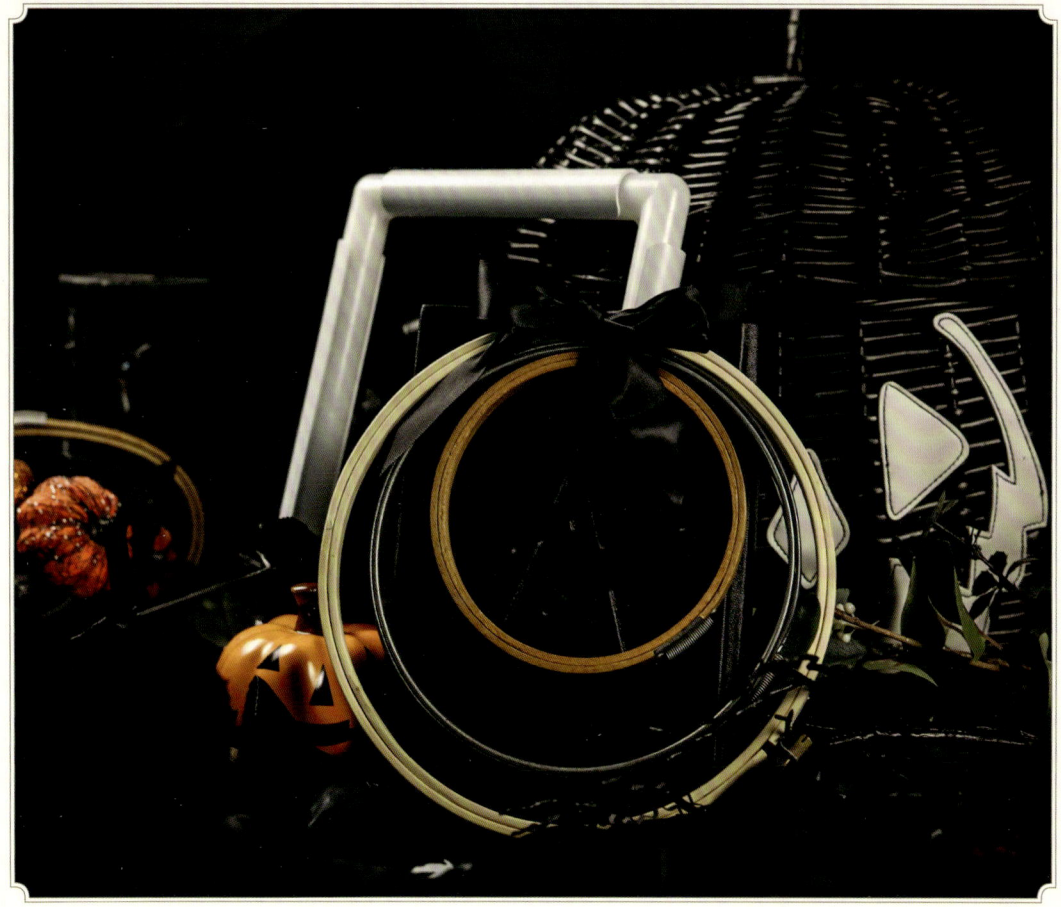

ABOVE Grime guards.

You can also hold your fabric with magnetic or binder clips. If there is still too much fabric to handle you may want to use a stand, which we will talk about next.

If the excess fabric isn't required for your finished piece, trim it off – there's no sense fighting with it! Life is already hard enough.

Stitching stands

A needlework or stitching stand holds a frame or a hoop so you don't have to. It works as a spare set of hands, leaving your own mitts free to stitch. There are many reasons to consider using a stand; you may have a large project or need to assuage body strains and pains, or maybe your familiar is always claiming your lap, leaving no room for your hoop.

Stitching stand options

There is an abundance of stand types available, so you are likely to find something to suit your particular needs.

★ **FLOOR STANDS:** stand independently on – you guessed it – the floor.
★ **LAP STANDS:** rest on your lap; your familiar would not approve.
★ **TABLE-TOP STANDS:** rest on a flat surface.
★ **CLAMP STANDS:** can be affixed to all kinds of things (I do not recommend a steering wheel – cross stitching and driving is dangerous, kids!).
★ **SEAT STANDS:** slip under your thigh and your body weight holds them in place.

I have tried all types of stands and my favorite is the floor stand, specifically the Lowery Workstand. It is considered the Lamborghini of cross stitch stands. This genius device was created in North Lincolnshire, England, in 1986 by Rosemary and Keith Lowery. They even offer customized work stands to suit personal needs, as everyone should be able to stitch, no matter their physical limitations.

- **FABRIC:** waterproof totes with some cedar balls to keep the moths from snacking.
- **KITTED PROJECTS:** dedicated project bags for each project, with all the necessary materials inside. Project keepers or binders are fantastic as well, and have space to hold your stitching, thread, needles, scissors, etc.
- **NEEDLES:** a needle book so I can return each needle size or type to its proper place once no longer needed, otherwise it is gone … perhaps forever.

GHOST TIP
Take breaks and stretch out your hands during long stitching sessions. If they begin to cramp up it is a sign to take a breather and rest your precious mitts.

Other useful accessories

- **SEAM RIPPER:** mistakes happen. Sometimes you become too involved in your latest binge watch, and before you know it you have made an oopsie in your project. Seam rippers are a necessary (evil) addition to your crafty box of tricks.
- **NEEDLE THREADER:** if you are having trouble threading your needle, grab yourself some threaders. They are small, looped devices that make threading a breeze. You slip the threader through the eye of the needle, put your floss in the threader loop and pull it through the eye. Spooktacular!
- **LIGHTING:** the weave of cross stitch fabric can be hard on the eyes if you don't have adequate lighting. A posable lamp is an excellent choice; my preferred tool is a neck or head light. Most of my stitching is done in the evenings and I enjoy not having to turn a bunch of lights on, especially the dreaded ceiling light. A focused light illuminates your project, allowing for a spooky, moody crafting session.

Storage and organization

Once you have entered the realm of cross stitch, storage quickly becomes a beast that you vanquish. Every stitcher's storage solutions are unique, so I am just going to cover how I personally store my bits and bobs.

The most important storage tip I will give you is to keep things out of direct sunlight for extended periods. I learned this the hard way with some ~~sun-bleached~~ sun-kissed threads. Protect your craft investment, stitch witches!

Storage suggestions

- **THREAD:** on bobbins in clear plastic cases, labeled with contents. As much as I would love a luxurious, aesthetically pleasing wooden case, I use my floss so frequently I need to be able to transport my entire color library easily while designing and color testing.

The Witchy Stitcher's guide to stitchcraft

How to read a cross stitch pattern

A cross stitch pattern is like a map that guides you. It tells you where to start stitching, what colors to use and how to determine the finished size of your masterpiece. The grid on a cross stitch chart corresponds to the grid created by the fabric's weave, with each square representing a single stitch. The combination of colors and symbols in squares (or symbols only, depending on chart style) indicate what color of floss to use in each square. I like to compare it to paint by numbers, but with thread.

There are two ways to begin a cross stitch; the first is to start in the middle and the second is to start from a corner (usually upper left). But first, let's get the fabric ready!

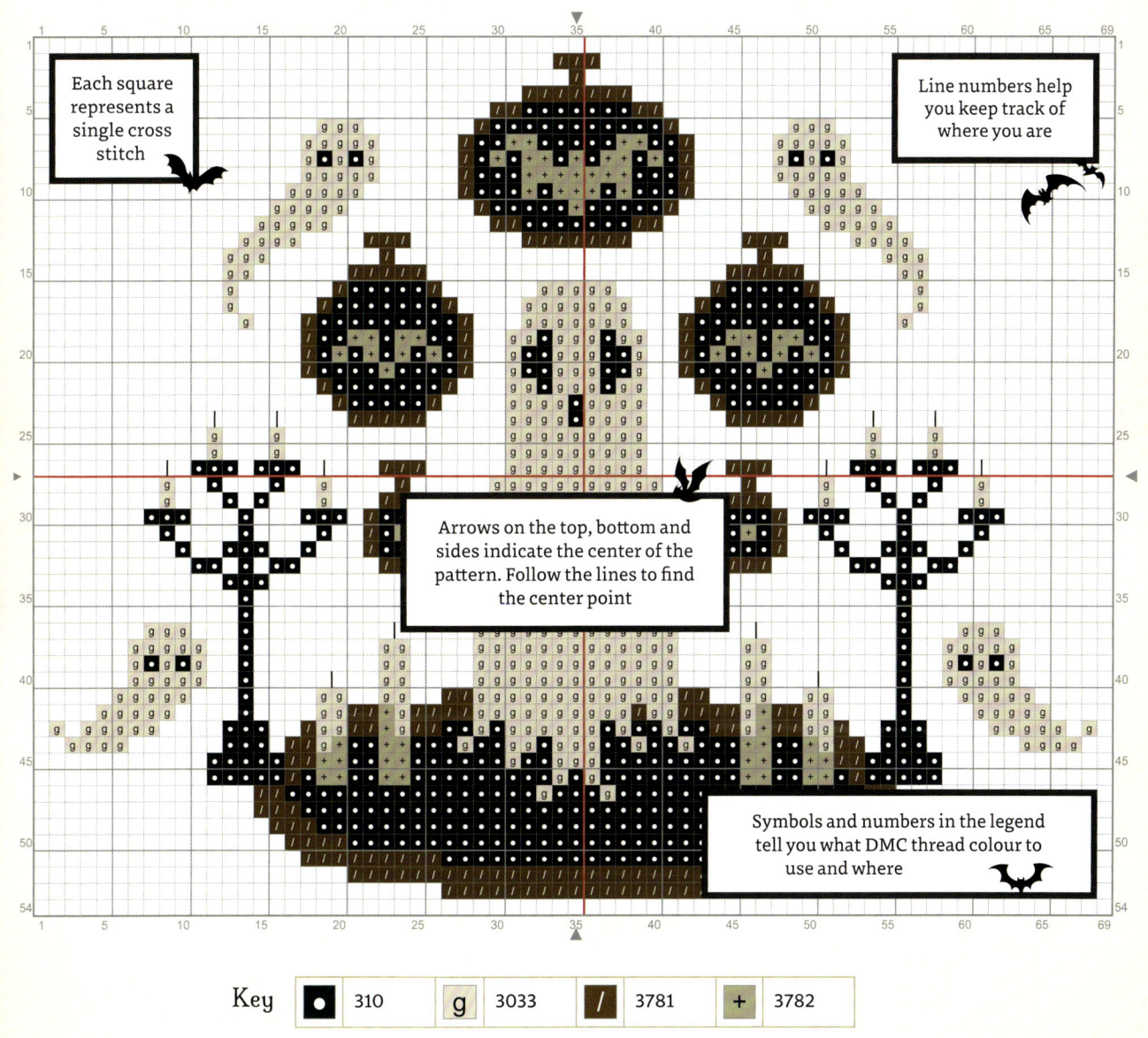

Each square represents a single cross stitch

Line numbers help you keep track of where you are

Arrows on the top, bottom and sides indicate the center of the pattern. Follow the lines to find the center point

Symbols and numbers in the legend tell you what DMC thread colour to use and where

Key | ● 310 | g 3033 | / 3781 | + 3782

How to prepare your fabric

Cross stitch patterns come with what is called a stitch count. This is found listed on your pattern, or it can be determined by the numbers along the sides of the chart. The stitch count is made up of the number of stitches horizontally and vertically in the design, and it relates directly to the finished size of your project.

The patterns throughout this grimoire list their finished sizes, but in the wild you may not have this information. You can calculate this yourself or use an online cross stitch calculator. I prefer to use the latter myself, because, you know, math, but I will teach you how to do it without internet hacks.

Information you need:

★ Stitch count (width x height, shown on the pattern)
★ The count (ct) of your fabric

For our example, we will be using this sample chart (see page 24 for the full chart).

The Haunted Parlor

STITCH COUNT: 69w x 54h
FABRIC: 14ct Aida

All you need to do is divide the number of stitches by the count of your fabric:

69 ÷ 14 = 4.9in (12.5cm)
54 ÷ 14 = 3.9in (10cm)

Finished stitch area = 4.9in wide x 3.9in high (12.5cm wide x 10cm high).

Now that we have sorted the space needed to stitch our thread masterpiece, we need to allow for a border and framing. I like to be generous with my borders so there is a lot of room for finishing and framing. I recommend at least 3–4in (7.5–10cm) around the stitched area. You can of course use a smaller border if you wish.

If you want 3in (7cm) of extra space around your design, add 6in (15cm) to both the width and height of your calculated fabric size. For this example, that would be:

4.9 + 6 = 10.9in
(12.5 + 15 = 27.5cm)
3.9 + 6 = 9.9in
(10 + 15 = 25cm)

My fabric for this ghostly creation would be 10.9 x 9.9in (27.5 x 25cm). You have some breathing room here, so you don't need to cut it exactly, as we have given ourselves an ample border.

THE WITCHY STITCHER'S GUIDE TO STITCHCRAFT

WHAT IF I'M USING EVENWEAVE OR LINEN?

If you are stitching over two threads on linen or evenweave fabric (see page 36 for an explanation of 'stitching over two'), you want to halve your fabric count before calculating. Let's say you are stitching on 32ct linen; divide 32 by 2 and then calculate. If you are stitching over one thread, then divide by 32.

69 ÷ 16 = 4.3in (11cm)
54 ÷ 16 = 3.4in (8.5cm)

You calculate the border and framing allowance in the same way as before, regardless of the count of your fabric.

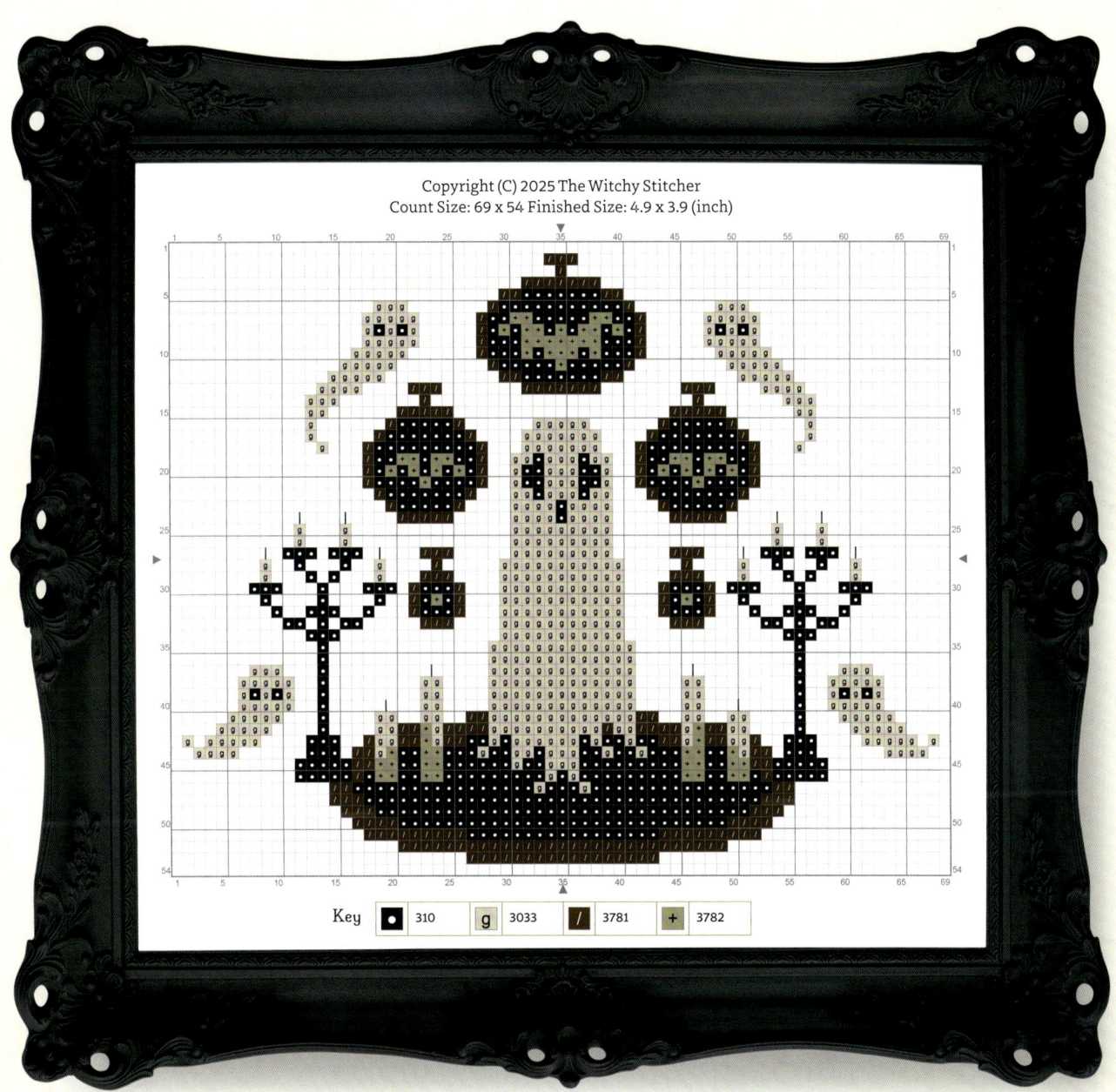

WANT TO STITCH THIS SAMPLE PROJECT? HERE ARE THE DETAILS!

FABRIC: 28ct Winter Wren by Fox & Rabbit Designs
COLORS: 4
STRANDS USED: 2
DIFFICULTY: Low
TOTAL STITCHES: 1,374

STITCH COUNT: 69w x 54h
FINISHED SIZE: on 28ct, stitched 2 over 2
WIDTH: 4.9in (12.5cm)
HEIGHT: 3.9in (10cm)

Thread

DMC THREAD	STITCHES	THREAD USED
310	550	½ skein
3033	499	½ skein
3781	255	¼ skein
3782	70	⅛ skein

Backstitching Details

DETAIL	DMC THREAD	STRANDS
Candle flames	310	2

I talk about finishing your project in a hoop or frame on pages 182–187.

Key: ● 310   g 3033   / 3781   + 3782

Protecting your fabric

Cross stitch fabric is woven, and these fabrics have an annoying tendency to fray when cut. Before you start stitching, it is a good idea to bind the edges, particularly if you are stitching a large project that will require lots of handling. To stop the fraying from pushing you into a meltdown, sew the edges with a zig-zag stitch (by hand or on your sewing machine) or use a Serger if you have one. If you don't want to sew the edges, you can also bind them with masking tape or a liquid sealant, both readily available at craft or sewing stores. Grime guards also help reduce fray, as the fabric is bundled up like a baby inside your guard.

You can choose just to go for it, but keep an eye on those edges in case they need an intervention.

GHOST TIP
If you are using masking tape, reduce the stickiness a bit before applying it to your fabric by sticking it to yourself a few times. This will reduce the chances of it pulling out some of the weave when you remove it.

How to prepare your hoop or frame

Using an embroidery hoop
To use a hoop, first loosen the screw and separate the two circles. Place the hoop without the screw on a flat surface. Lay the fabric over it, making sure the fabric is centered. Place the hoop with the screw over the fabric and press it down. Gently pull the fabric taut as you tighten the screw on the top. Don't pull the fabric too tight or it will distort the weave. You want just enough that you get a soft drum sound when you tap on the center.

Using a frame
To use a snap frame, lay your fabric over the frame, making sure it is centered. Attach the clamps to the bars, with your fabric between the frame and the clamps. After all the clamps have been added, twist them away from each other. This will stretch and secure your fabric.

I favor snap frames because they hold the fabric under tension for longer, and the square/rectangle shape is more comfortable to hold for longer periods.

GHOST TIP
When using a snap frame, I place a strip of felt between the fabric and the clamps. The extra padding helps to avoid squished stitches and prevents the clamps from marking the fabric.

Bring out yer thread!

Cut a length of thread about 18in (46cm) long. If the thread is much longer than this, it is likely to get knotted as you stitch, causing stitcher's rage and the risk of thrown projects. I am, however, a lazy hag and I do gamble with long strands – I don't like to change my thread often and usually just witch up and deal with the knots.

Embroidery floss is made up of six strands of thread. Depending on the fabric you are using, you will typically stitch with two strands at a time, although with 11ct aida, three strands is the norm. If you like a fuller stitch, by all means throw in an extra strand! Many stitchers actually prefer to use three strands.

1. To separate out a single thread, hold the floss with one hand and tap the top of the thread. This separates the strands a bit so it's easier to grasp one.
2. Gently and slowly pull one strand up and out while holding the rest of thread around the top. Even if you need more than one strand, pull one at a time or you risk creating a tangled mess that reeks of regret.

Ready your needle and anchor your thread

I don't recommend making a knot in the tail-end; it can leave visible lumps in the final piece, or show through your fabric. The most common starting methods are the traditional start or loop start. My preferred method is the loop start, but we will cover both.

If you dislike either of these methods and want to keep making your knots, you do you, boo! I don't like a lot of rules in my creative spaces, and I wouldn't want that for you either. Just have fun.

Traditional start

Cut your desired length of floss or the recommended 18in (46cm) and separate out the number of strands you will be using. Holding both strands together, thread one end through the needle.

1. Bring the needle up from the back of your fabric to the front at the point you plan to begin stitching. Leave about an inch (2.5cm) of thread at the back. You will cover the tail with your stitches as you work, to secure it.
2. Make your first half stitch (see page 31). Be sure to hold on to that tail so it doesn't slip through!
3. Start the second half of the stitch by bringing the needle through the hole directly above the one you last used, from the back of the fabric. Before you pull it tight, flip over your fabric to make sure the thread tail will be trapped by the stitch.
4. Continue stitching and trapping the loose tail under your stitching. Three to five stitches is plenty to hold the tail in place (Steps 4 and 5). Snip off the excess.

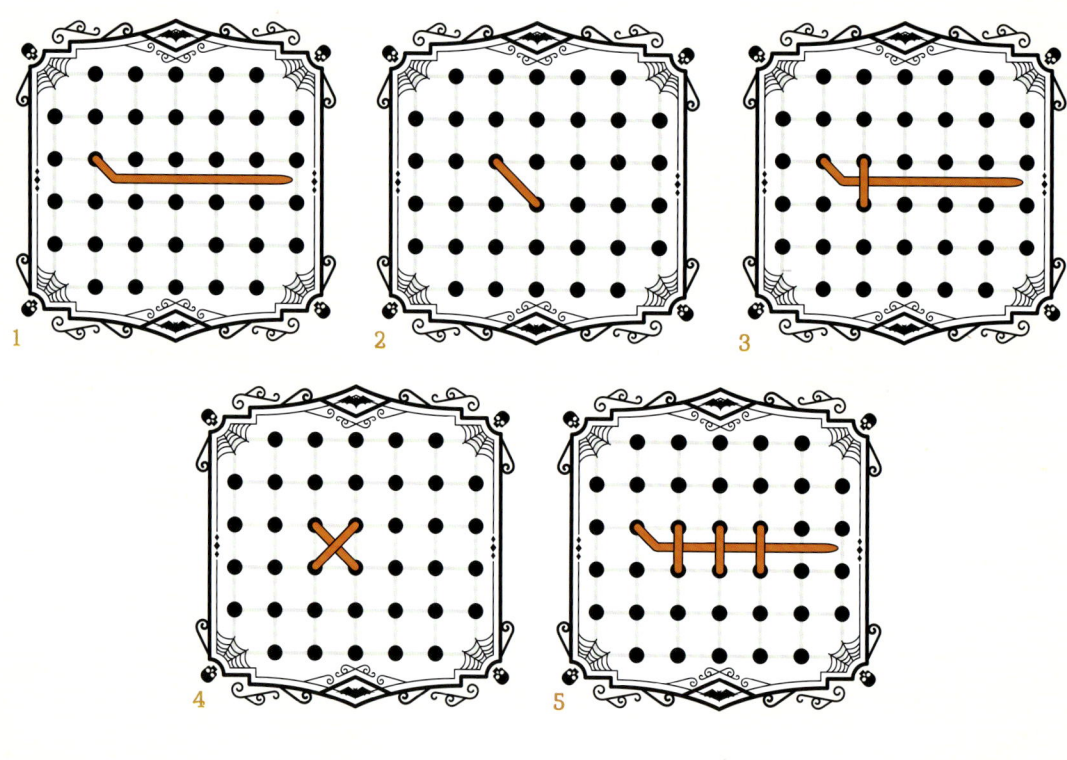

Loop start

This method is for a two-strand loop start. You can do a three-strand loop start, but because this grimoire features only two-stranded designs, we won't cover that here.

Cut a length of floss twice the length that you will be using; e.g., if you are going with the recommended 18in (46cm), cut your floss to 36in (92cm).

1. Separate out one strand of floss and fold it in half so the ends meet up.
2. Thread the two single ends of the strands through the needle; the other end of the thread will form a loop.
3. Bring your needle up from the back of your fabric to the front at the point you plan to begin stitching. Leave a bit of the loop at the back.
4. Make your first half stitch, taking care not to pull your thread all the way through.
5. Flip your project over and slip your needle through the loop.
6. Pull gently to tighten. The loop will lie flat against the back of the fabric and your thread will now be held in place!

Starting your stitchcraft

How to start from the middle

This is my preferred technique, as you aren't required to do any measuring beyond making sure your fabric is the right size.

1. Small arrows are located along the edges of the pattern, which mark the center of the design on each axis. Choose an arrow from the top or bottom and one from the left or right, and follow their paths until they meet; this intersection is the center of the pattern (see page 21 for reference).
2. Pick a stitch closest to the middle of the chart and match it up with the center of your fabric.
3. To find the center of your fabric, fold it in half horizontally and then vertically. Pinch the center of your folds to mark them with a crease. You can also place a pin in the center or make a quick stitch so as to not lose track of the center while you place the fabric in your hoop or frame.
4. I usually have my needle threaded and ready, so I can pop it in the center for my first stitch and away I go!

How to start from a corner

This one requires a trusty ruler or measuring tape. As you have already prepared your fabric, you need to make sure you don't start within the border area.

1. Measure the amount you allowed for your border from the edges of your fabric; e.g., let's say you chose the recommended 3in (7.5cm) as I suggest, measure 3in in from the top and left edges.
2. Where these measurements meet is your starting point in relation to the corner of the pattern.
3. You will likely need to count down and/or over to your first stitch.

No matter where you start stitching from, the most important thing is that your fabric is the correct size. You don't want to run out of fabric or find your pattern is off-center, throwing off your border. It is truly horrifying to realize you have miscalculated only after you have spent hours carefully stitching.

GHOST TIP
Make sure your fabric is orientated to match your chart before you begin. If the design is roughly square, it won't matter, but if it is landscape or portrait, be sure your fabric and pattern match!

Single stitches

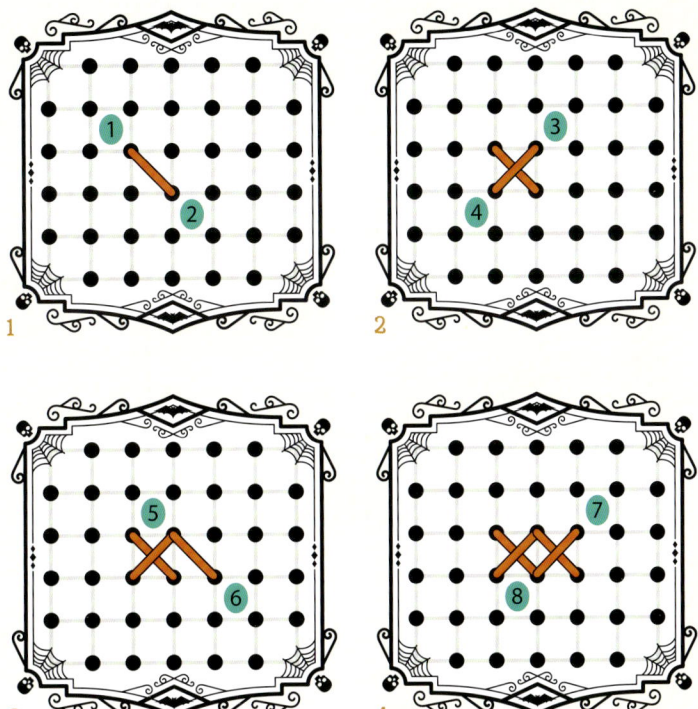

For single stitches, you make one X at a time. You don't have to follow the diagram numbers exactly; you can orientate your stitches as you like, as long as you follow the steps below. The most important thing is that you make your stitches the same way every time. If your top crosses lie in different directions, your finished product can look less uniform.

1 Come up at 1 and go down at 2. This stage gives you a half stitch.
2 Come up at 3 and go down at 4.
3 Repeat! (Steps 3 and 4)

You can use any start method you prefer for single stitches.

Stitching in rows

Stitching in rows can be much faster than doing single stitches. Instead of making each full cross stitch individually, row stitching involves creating a length of half stitches and then turning around and making your top crosses to finish the row.

1 Create a row of half stitches, following the numbers 1–8 as shown.
2 Turn around and finish those stitches, following the numbers 9 and 10 (Step 2) and 11–16 (Step 3).

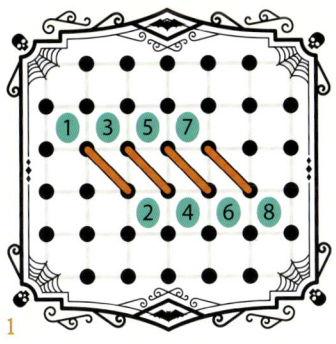

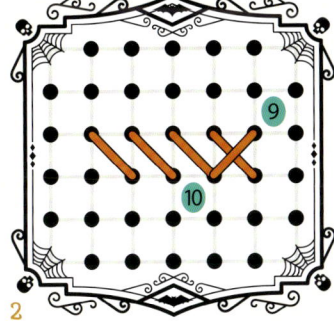

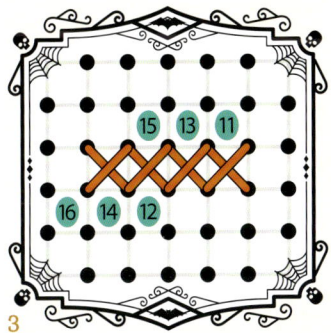

Specialty stitches

Backstitching

Backstitching is very common in cross stitch patterns. It can be used to outline areas and add detail. It is called 'backstitching' because you work backward, then jump ahead, then work backward again, and repeat. It is like a sewing version of connect the dots.

1. Come up through the back of the fabric at 1 and go down in 2.
2. Come up at 3.
3. Go down at 4, the same hole as you went down in 2.
4. Your stitches should rest on top of your single cross stitches, not underneath them.

You can easily change the direction your stitches are going by working to the right, left or diagonally.

GHOST TIP
Try not to carry your backstitching over too many squares – my rule is no more than three – as it can become loose and sag. That said, you may have to use more squares for a special situation or detail.

Pinhead stitch

Pinhead or 'pin' stitches are perfect for scattered standalone stitches. You can carry your thread without stopping and restarting (despite what the 'rules' say), but there are times when the distance between stitches is either too far, or you don't want to risk being able to see the carried threads from the front of your project. This is where pinhead stitches swoop in to save the day!

This method works on all fabric types, but note that if you are using aida you will have to force the needle through the fabric weave as there are no ready-made holes at A, B and C as there are with evenweave or linen.

Pinhead stitches are best started with the loop start method (see page 29). Fig. 1 shows the locations of each number for reference during the process.

Fig.1

1   Create a single cross stitch.
2   Coming up from the back of the fabric enter through A and go down at B behind the crossed strands of your single stitch.
3   Come up again through the back of the fabric through C and go down again at B, behind the crossed strands of your single stitch. Pull slightly to tighten and snip at the back of the project.

NOTE: The edges of the A, B and C stitches will show a little at the front of your fabric.

French knot

French knots have a bit of a reputation for being difficult, frustrating and the cause of many an abandoned project, but with a little practice you can master them. Explaining how to do them in picture form might not be enough to visualize the process. I highly recommend finding video instructions if you are struggling.

This stitch is done with two hands: one to hold the needle and the other to wrap and hold the thread.

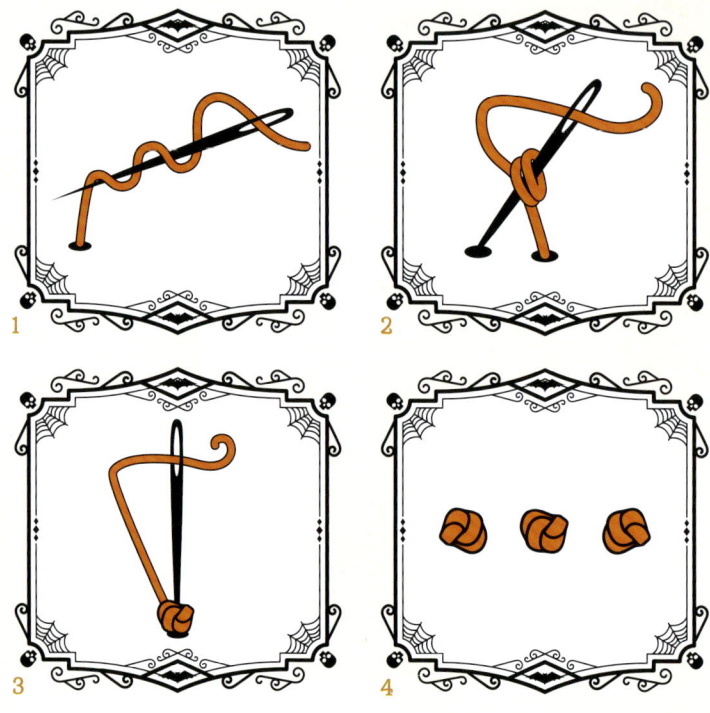

1. Bring your needle up from the back where you would like the French knot to be, and wrap the thread around the needle 2–3 times.
2. You will be going down in a separate hole from where you began – if you go down in the same space your knot will disappear. With aida you can make a new hole in between two existing ones.
3. Pull on the tail thread slightly while simultaneously pushing the needle through the knot and out the back of your project.
4. Celebrate your perfect French knot … hopefully.

GHOST TIP
If you make a mistake, it is perfectly acceptable to cast your project across the room. Just be mindful of small children, pets and blissfully unaware spirits in its trajectory.

¼ and ¾ stitches

These stitches are not used in this grimoire, and I rarely use them. They are quite difficult to make, regardless of fabric type. To make sure my designs are accessible to all skill levels I tend to stick to the most common stitches, but knowledge is power, so here is what they look like.

¼ stitch

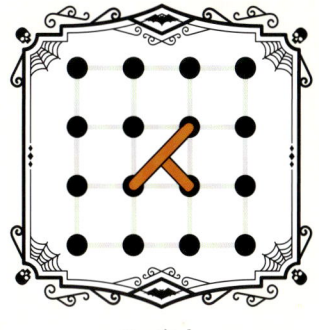
¾ stitch

Railroading

Railroading is completely optional, but if you find your stitches are messier than you would like, or you are getting uneven coverage, definitely give it a go. Years ago, I did this by accident and thought I was a genius, only to discover I was just uninformed.

Railroading is a simple and effective technique that forces your threads to lie flat, giving a cleaner and more even appearance. As you stitch, your thread naturally twists, which can make your stitches look unruly or wonky. Glow in the dark and metallic fibers tend to twist more frequently, so this method is very useful if you're using them. One less well known advantage of railroading is coverage, as it allows the thread to sit better, and makes the stitch look fuller.

There are two ways to railroad your stitches. The first is by splitting your threads, and the second is with a special accessory called a laying tool. For simplicity's sake, we are going to cover the thread-splitting method, because no extra tools are required.

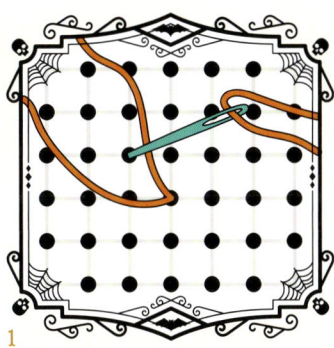
1

2

1 Start your stitching as usual, coming up from the back.

2 Before going back down, you are going to split your threads and put your needle in between the two strands.

Very simply, every time you go down through your fabric, you will insert the needle between the threads and split them.

Finishing your thread

1. To finish off your thread, slide the needle behind four or five stitches at the back of your project.
2. Pull the needle through and trim off the excess thread.

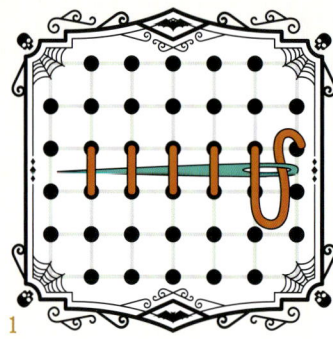
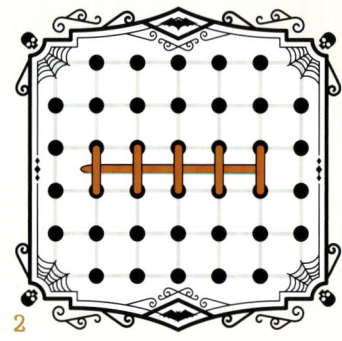

1   2

Stitching 'over 1' or 'over 2'

Generally, aida is stitched over one square and evenweave and linen are stitched over two, although they can also be stitched over one. Are you lost yet? Let's break it all down, with pictures!

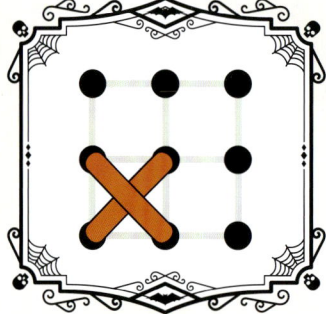

Aida, 2 over 1: Using two strands of thread, stitch over one square. No holes are skipped.

Evenweave/linen, 1 over 1: Using one strand of thread, stitch over one square. No holes are skipped.

Evenweave/linen, 2 over 2: Using two strands of thread, stitch over two squares. You skip a hole each time both vertically and horizontally.

GHOST TIP

When you are done stitching for the day, loosen the tension of your hoop or frame. Leaving your fabric under tension for extended periods can cause hoop burn – an unsightly ring where the frame was. It can be difficult to get out of your project, but not impossible; some steam and a bit of vinegar work wonders.

Bookmark tutorial

Each pattern section of this stitcher's grimoire begins with a bookmark design. You can buy pre-made bookmarks online, from sewing shops or from many small businesses who create them. It is also pretty easy to make your own. There is a multitude of ways to make them too – no rules. You can use a sewing machine, hand-stitch, or even just glue them!

BOOKMARK TUTORIAL

How I make my bookmarks

I begin my bookmarks as I do any other cross stitch, by using a frame. The first step is the easiest of them all; simply stitch your project and don't worry about the finished size just yet. Leave yourself ample room to stitch comfortably.

Materials needed
- ★ Your finished cross stitch
- ★ Scissors
- ★ Ruler
- ★ Needle
- ★ Extra thread for backstitching
- ★ Iron
- ★ Tweezers

1 Trim your bookmark leaving roughly ½–¾in (1.2–1.9cm) at the top and bottom and ¼in (0.6cm) on each side. For this tutorial, and because I'm using 14ct aida, I left four grid holes at each side and nine at the top and bottom.

2 Fold and press the sides with an iron; leave the top and bottom as is for now. When folding the edges try to keep them as straight as possible. The grid holes should line up on the front and folded edge.

3 Backstitch around the stitched area, making sure to stitch through the folded edge. I like to use a sharper needle, as it is easier to push through the double layer.

4 Using tweezers, pull the tiny horizontal thread strands out along the top and bottom. You can trim these tassel-like edges or leave them any length you like! Pulling these strands will stop your fabric from fraying, and it looks so cute. For really starchy fabric this can be tougher to do, as the threads are quite stubborn. Poking a sturdy needle through and lifting the strands can work much better.

5 Put your new fancy bookmark in your latest spooky story!

OPTIONAL: Adding backing. You can add a piece of felt or fabric to the back if you wish. I like to leave mine bare. I find something so interesting about the backs of cross stitch and prefer to leave it uncovered, but you can do whatever you like!

Using a pre-made bookmark

The most important thing is obtaining a bookmark that is the correct size for your pattern, because they come in a variety of sizes and colors. Once you have your bookmark, simply start stitching! Find the center and stitch your project as you would a large piece of fabric in a frame. The only difference is you will likely be stitching in hand. It can be a bit tricky, but it is absolutely doable! You can use a small frame to stitch some of the design, but this becomes almost impossible when you reach the top and bottom edges of the bookmark.

It is important to note that even with the wide array of pre-made sizes available, you might not find one to suit your pattern. Be prepared to edit the chart a bit to match your available stitching area.

Book of Spells Bookmark

FABRIC: 14ct Grey Aida by Burlap Fabrics
COLORS: 2
STRANDS USED: 2
DIFFICULTY: Low
TOTAL STITCHES: 1,692

Thread

DMC THREAD	STITCHES	THREAD USED
■ 310	1,297	¾ skein
▨ 3865	395	½ skein

STITCH COUNT: 31w x 113h
FINISHED SIZE: on 14ct, stitched 2 over 1
WIDTH: 2.21in (5.5cm)
HEIGHT: 8.07in (20.5cm)

Backstitching Details

DETAIL	DMC THREAD	STRANDS
Pentacle	▨ 3865	2
Skull teeth	■ 310	2

Key

■	310
♥	3865

Being 'extra'

Beads and embellishments

There are many ways to add a little extra spice to your stitchcraft. One of the most popular is to add beads instead of stitches. They are a wonderful addition to your finished piece and add some dimension and shimmer. There are no limits on embellishing. You can add charms, 3D objects, embroidery-style stitches and more! Let your imagination run rampant and have some fun when creativity strikes. Adding beads and embellishments should be the last step before completing your project – you don't want anything to get squished or broken.

BEING 'EXTRA'

How to add beads

Materials needed

★ Seed beads: size 11/0 is the most common size for cross stitch (I use Mill Hill beads)
★ Beading needle (or a needle small enough to go through a bead)
★ Bead mat or tray (anything will do, really)
★ Beading thread or a single strand of thread to match your fabric

1. Bring the threaded needle up through the back of your fabric in the bottom left of the 'square' where you want your bead to rest. Pass the needle through the bead and go down through the top right of the 'square'.

2. Bring the needle up from the bottom right.

3. Twist the bead a little and push the needle from right to left through the center again. Go down in the top left hole of the fabric. Bead secured!

The easiest way to add beads is to think about making regular single stitches, but each time you come up through the fabric, you put your needle and thread through the bead on the way back down into the fabric.

As with single stitches you can do this in a different order than explained, as long as each bead is completed the same way. Alternatively, you can do a half stitch instead of a full stitch, with half stitches the beads will be on an angle, while with a full stitch they will sit straight.

ABOVE Beadwork on Till Death (to be found within this grimoire on page 172).

~ BEING 'EXTRA' ~

Antiquing your cross stitch

In many of my finished pieces, I use paint to get a streaked antique gothic look. The idea came to me when I was admiring old tombstones at a local cemetery. I immediately wanted to incorporate this into my cross stitch. To me, the streaked letters signify beauty born of time and nature.

Materials needed

* Watercolor paint
* Paintbrushes
* Water
* Rag/paper towel

I like to use a variety of brush sizes when doing this nerve-racking process. Filling large areas with a small brush doesn't give a very smooth result, and using a big brush for fine details isn't my idea of a fun art experience. I would rather cut onions in a tiny windowless room.

For the watercolor paint, any brand will do. Surprisingly, I find that the cheaper paints work better for fabric – win! I mainly use black pigments for this, but you can use any color your heart desires.

Before you attempt this on your finished piece, I recommend testing on a spare piece of fabric, or the edges of your finished piece that will be hidden by a frame. Your cross stitch just took you many precious hours to create, so you want to feel confident when brush hits fabric. The process can take some getting used to, but with a bit of practice and patience you can add an extra dimension and intrigue to your work, and really give it that extra 'wow' factor.

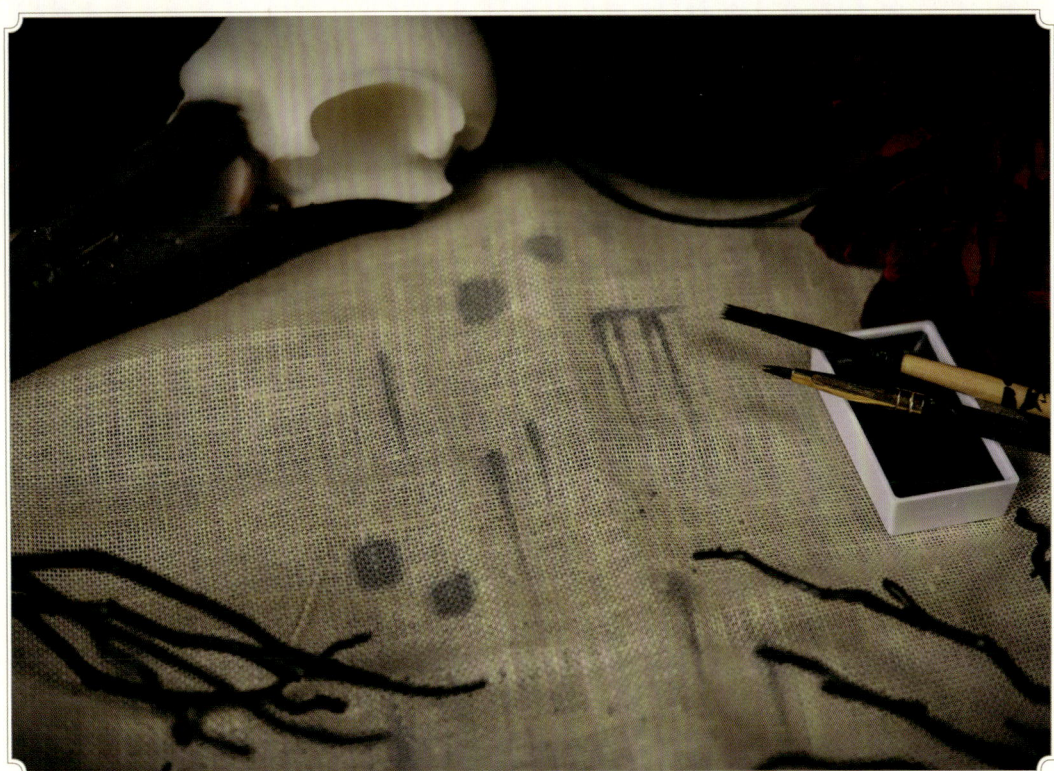

ABOVE Testing my paint.

1. Wash (if needed) and iron your work; you won't be able to wash it again after you paint. I talk about washing your fabric on page 183.

2. Breathe. You are about to actually paint your cross stitch. I remember the first time I was about to try this; I was shaking like a fragile little leaf.

3. Dilute your paint with water, dabbing any excess off on your rag. Start off with a light wash to see how it will absorb into the fabric. How you apply the paint to the fabric depends on what look you are going for.

For the streaked look, start at the base of the element and pull down streaks of the watered-down paint, trailing off as you go. Keep your paint light and don't add too much too soon – you can't undo it! Start with one layer on all areas where you wish to use this effect, then let it dry.

4. Once the first layer dries (you can use a hair dryer to speed it up), you can go back in and darken areas to create more depth and contrast. This effect takes a lot of time and patience.

I usually do around four to six layers of paint, letting it dry fully in between coats. Paint looks darker when it is wet, so let it dry completely before calling it done.

5. Finishing your work. If you need to iron it again, use the lowest heat possible and no water; the paint could bleed if you use steam. I like to let my piece rest for at least a few hours before completely finishing or framing it. Sometimes I even paint it after it is framed!

BELOW Painting in progress.

ABOVE Before.   ABOVE After.

Fabric magic

With a bit of time and a few supplies you can make your own unique, custom fabric; you don't have to buy it pre-made. There are many ways to dye fabric, the most common being with fabric dye, or natural dyes like tea or coffee. If you want a more primitive and antique look, tea/coffee is the easiest way. For color-specific or multi-tonal looks, use fabric dye. The sky truly is the limit; I have even seen folks use Kool Aid or avocado pits. You can imagine my shock when I learned that avocado pits dye fabric pink!

BEING 'EXTRA'

How to dye with coffee and tea

There are many ways to approach dyeing cross stitch fabric with coffee and/or tea and this is just how I tackle it. I prefer to use coffee and tea together as I find it gives the best balance of warm and cool tones. My 'recipe' is enough for a fat quarter approx. 18 x 21in (45.75 x 53cm) but you can multiply the quantities for larger batches of fabric.

Coffee and tea are both natural acid dyes – just as they can stain your clothes, they can permanently stain your cross stitch canvas. Black teas work best for dyeing due to their high levels of tannins. Fruit-based teas also work but tend to fade over time as they have lower tannin levels.

Natural dyes have the added bonus of being food-safe, and using them does not require dedicated tools, unlike with chemical fabric dyes. You can bake your delicious sweet treats on the same tray as you bake your fabric.

Materials needed

★ Fat quarter of light-colored cross stitch fabric
★ 3 cups of strong coffee (instant or leftovers)
★ 4 teabags (preferably black tea)
★ 1 tbsp of salt
★ Cauldron (large bowl or pot)
★ Tongs
★ Water
★ Oven
★ Baking sheet
★ Iron
★ Parchment paper
★ Optional: 1 tsp cinnamon; a towel

1 Prepare your coffee and tea. I use either leftover coffee or brew strong 8oz cups of instant coffee. Old and instant coffee give richer results. Steep your tea in 2 cups of water for a minimum of 15 minutes. Pour into your cauldron and mix in 1 tbsp of salt. The salt helps the dye penetrate the fibers of the fabric.

OPTIONAL STEP: Add 1 tsp of cinnamon – it helps dye the fabric but mostly it smells wonderful and the scent will stick around after, too. Dreamy.

FUN WITCHY STITCHER FACT
I love making my pieces look vintage and stained. Sometimes I even dye my projects with coffee and tea after I have finished stitching them. As I'm sure you can imagine, this is a bit scary … but you can get some wild and unique results!

3 Let it rest for between an hour to overnight: the longer you leave your fabric, the darker it will be. If you're leaving your fabric for more than an hour, move it around every one or two hours so that all of the fabric gets some dye. Check it now and then to see if you have reached your desired color. Bear in mind that the wet fabric will look darker than its true color. If dyeing overnight then just leave it – don't set an alarm or anything silly like that. This is a really organic process so don't stress over it! It's almost impossible to ruin the fabric. Heck, I have left fabric for a couple days and it still turned out stunning.

2 Wet your fabric with plain water and gently squeeze out the excess but don't wring it out. Submerge it in your dye-bath – you don't need to wait for the cauldron to cool fully. If you want a uniform color, use weights to hold your fabric down; for a marbled and unique look, let bits of the fabric poke out of the dye (it will do this naturally). Another method is to scrunch it up and put elastic bands around it as if tie dying. This will give more stark and detailed color variations with nearly white areas beside deep browns.

ABOVE Overnight dye – before baking.

4 Once you are happy with the saturation (or close to it), it's time to bake! This will give the color more depth and darken it a few shades. To do this, lay it on a baking sheet and scrunch it up like shown above. Add some extra liquid to your fabric from your dye-bath, if you don't then it will burn!

Bake at 200°F (93°C) for 15–30 minutes, checking it often, and don't leave it unattended. If the fabric begins to dry out too much then add a bit more of the dyed liquid so that you don't fry it. You will start to see bits of the fabric darken so move your fabric around to get even coverage throughout the baking process.

BEING 'EXTRA'

5 Rinse and dry. Remove your fabric from the oven then, using your tongs, place it in the sink. Rinse with cool water and lay to dry on an old towel, or hang it outside. It will likely stain your towel, so choose wisely. The dye process can make it a crinkly mess so, once dry, sandwich your fabric between two pieces of parchment paper to protect your surface and then iron it. You can also wet the fabric to help remove stubborn creases.

Here are some samples of what fabric magic looks like after one hour, three hours and overnight.

ABOVE One hour – elastic band method.

ABOVE Three hours.

ABOVE Overnight.

GHOST TIP
Fabric types each absorb dye differently and will give you unique results: aida tends to dye darker, and linen dyes lighter. You can adjust processing times or dye strengths to obtain your desired results. It is all about playing around and having fun!

Stitching vernacular

As you immerse yourself in the world of cross stitch, you will come across many strange and unusual incantations. I was often puzzled and became close friends with Google in an attempt to make sense of what everyone was on about. To save you the trouble, I have compiled a list of often-used stitch slang.

STITCHING VERNACULAR

ANCHOR: a brand of embroidery thread. 100% cotton.

BAP: Big Ass Project.

BOBBIN/BOBBINATE: Bobbins hold your thread; to bobbinate is to wind your thread onto bobbins.

DMC: a brand of embroidery thread. 100% cotton.

CXC: a brand of embroidery thread. Cotton/polyester blend.

CONE OF DOOM: Large cone of DMC 310, a necessity when working on Witchy Stitcher patterns.

CROW: Craft Room Organization; exists for some and not at all for others.

CONFETTI: single stitches of different colors in one area. Looks like confetti being thrown.

CT: count; the count of fabric.

FLOSS: embroidery thread or stranded cotton.

FLOSS DROPS: hold thread instead of using a bobbin.

FROG/FROGGING: when you've made a mistake (the horror!) and have to rip out some of your stitches; comes from the sound frogs make ('rip it, rip it').

FO: Finished Object. Stitching completed but not framed or fully finished.

FFO: Finally Finished Object, Fully Finished Object or Finally Framed Object.

FLOSSTUBE: YouTube channels that focus on fiber arts, primarily cross stitch.

FS: Forgotten Stash.

GITD: Glow in the dark thread.

KIT UP: Obtain supplies for your intended pattern/chart.

LNS: Local Needlecraft Shop.

MCBAP: Massively Complicated Big Ass Project.

OAP: Old Abandoned Project.

ONS: Online Needlecraft Shop.

OOP: Out Of Print.

ORT: Old Raggedy Threads or Orphaned Random Threads. ORT also means 'a scrap'. These are the small bits of thread left over from stitching. Many people save them and use them to fill jars or ornaments to honor their year of stitching.

PATTERN STASH: your hoard of cross stitch patterns.

PK: Pattern Keeper; a digital pattern markup app.

RAK: Random Act of Kindness; cross stitchers may give away surplus threads, fabric and physical patterns. Nothing is expected in return.

SAL: Stitch-a-Long; projects that are broken down into several parts where the pattern for each part is released at regular intervals and many stitchers join in, stitching each part at the same time. I host SALs often!

SLUB: a natural imperfection in linen fabric.

STASH: your hoard of cross stitch supplies (fabric, thread, etc.).

STITCH BUDDY: any familiar (pet), stuffed animal, or even a human that sits with you (or on you) when stitching.

TOAD: Trashed Object Abandoned in Disgust; enough said.

THE DEVIL'S HAIR: metallic threads; often unruly and difficult to work with.

THREAD CHICKEN: the game of 'is there enough thread to finish this area?'

THREAD GLOSS/WAX: used to tame unruly threads, great for The Devil's Hair.

UFO: Unfinished Object; sometimes also named this because it went flying at some point.

WIP: Work in Progress.

WTF: Waiting to Finish; not what you thought, hey?

> How to use these in a sentence: 'I'm so mad that I had to frog my SAL WIP, I might have to turn it into a TOAD. Maybe I will just go to my LNS to kit up a new chart and grab more devil's hair and add to my pattern stash.'

Patterns

Greetings, fellow ghouls and goblins! Welcome to the pattern grimoire entry haunted by witchy, gothic, Halloween and spooky holiday design offerings. Whether you are a baby stitch witch or a seasoned stitch sorcerer, this bewitching selection of patterns offers a little something for everyone.

Each section begins with a bookmark, as these are great for beginners. They are smaller pieces and will take the least amount of time to complete.

These designs use a variety of fabrics, but they are all compatible with any count from 11 to 52. Use whatever you desire and are most comfortable with. If you like the examples shown in this book, you are in luck! Each pattern comes with a full list of the supplies used to create it. Many are from fellow small businesses in the stitchy cosmos.

Now, grab your needle and thread, summon your stitching spirits and let's embark on a spooky stitching adventure together!

For the coven

Witchy patterns with a touch of darkness

We commence the pattern section of this grimoire with a collection of magical and witchy designs. Fiber arts on their own possess qualities that align directly with witchcraft itself: the meditative practice of cross stitch leans into spell work; every tool is an invocation of our desire; every stitch is an act of purpose and intent. The act of creation itself is magic. Artists take raw materials, purpose, time and skill and transform them into something tangible that didn't exist before. Yes, I make the patterns, but you are the ones that make the true magic and bring them to life. Whether you are a practitioner of the craft or simply drawn to the beauty and mystique of its imagery, this section offers a meaningful and inviting collection of witch-themed offerings.

FOR THE COVEN

Witchy Bookmark

Mark your place in your grimoire with this occult-themed bookmark. Whether you are a believer in the supernatural or simply drawn to the dark, the mystifying oracle is an image of great significance in the witchy and gothic communities.

It is believed that the Ouija board was born of the American nineteenth century obsession with spiritualism, and the belief that the dead are able to communicate with the living, although objects similar to the 'talking board' date back as far as 551 BCE. Wherever it may have originated, its intriguing look and other-worldly purpose cemented its place in the world of gothic imagery.

The double-sided candle has a few meanings. Candle magic is a core element of witchcraft and is an ancient way of manifesting and empowering your intentions. 'Burning the candle at both ends' means to overextend yourself, leading to exhaustion. Use this as a reminder to slow down, rest and take some time for yourself.

Not sure how to make a bookmark? Check out the tutorial on page 38.

Pattern details

FABRIC: 14ct Black Aida by Zweigart
COLORS: 6
STRANDS USED: 2
DIFFICULTY: Low
TOTAL STITCHES: 871

STITCH COUNT: 33w x 118h
FINISHED SIZE: on 14ct, stitched 2 over 1
WIDTH: 2.36in (6cm)
HEIGHT: 8.43in (21.5cm)

Thread

DMC THREAD	STITCHES	THREAD USED
310	17	⅛ skein
677	406	½ skein
728	100	⅛ skein
780	60	⅛ skein
782	83	⅛ skein
3852	205	¼ skein

Backstitching Details

DETAIL	DMC THREAD	STRANDS
Pentacle	310	2

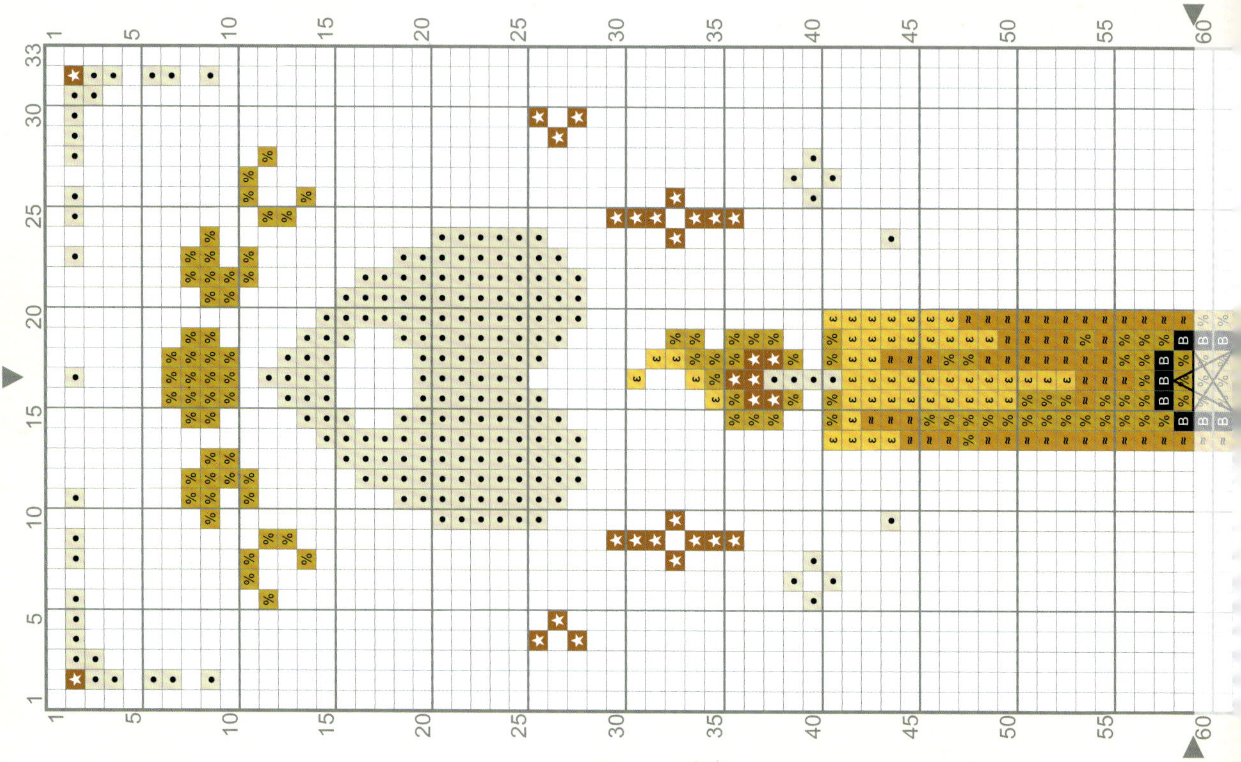

Key

B	310
•	677
ɛ	728
★	780
≈	782
%	3852

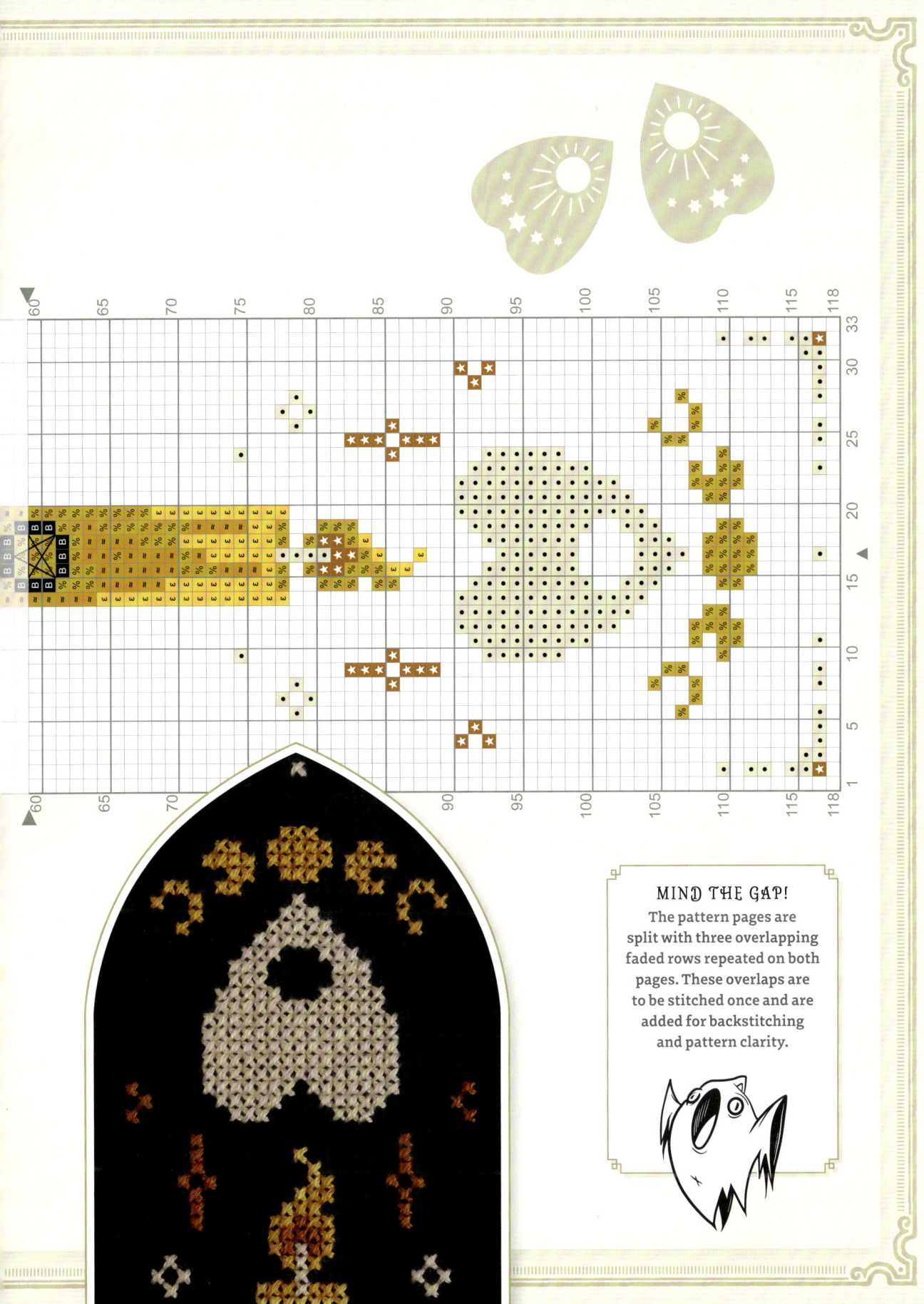

FOR THE COVEN

Bat Coven

Adorn your hallowed walls with this dapper and delicate coven of chiroptera! Bat Coven is a twist on the spooky reputation of these winged creatures of the night, transforming them into charming, well-dressed witches straight out of an era of elegance. Imagine them casting a spell with a flick of their wings, sipping on blood-red potions and soaring through the midnight skies.

Victorian elegance and charm oozes from this triptych of witchy bat comrades. I wonder what their covenstead looks like? It's doubtful that jars of bat wings line their apothecary walls – I suspect 'ear of human' is more likely to feature.

Don't be surprised if you find yourself under their spell, stitching long into the night. Embrace the magic and let the Bat Coven lead you on a stitching journey into the dark.

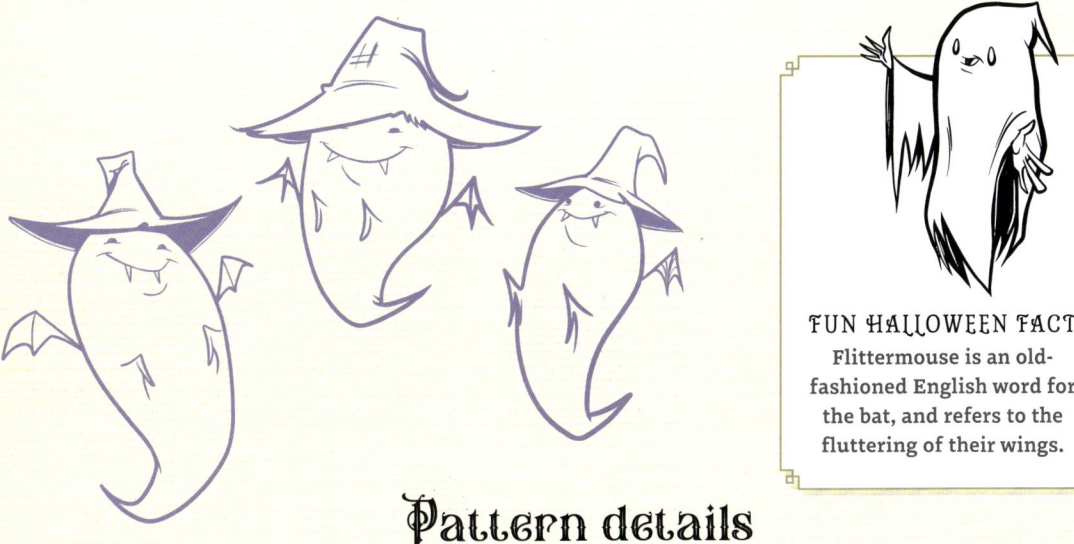

FUN HALLOWEEN FACT
Flittermouse is an old-fashioned English word for the bat, and refers to the fluttering of their wings.

Pattern details

FABRIC: 30ct Boleyn Linen by The Primitive Hare
COLORS: 4
STRANDS USED: 2
DIFFICULTY: Low
TOTAL STITCHES: 3,999

STITCH COUNT: 115w x 92h
FINISHED SIZE: on 30ct, stitched 2 over 2
WIDTH: 7.67in (19.5cm) HEIGHT: 6.13in (15.5cm)
FINISHED SIZE: on 14ct, stitched 2 over 1
WIDTH: 8.21in (20.8cm) HEIGHT: 6.57in (16.7cm)

Thread

DMC THREAD	STITCHES	THREAD USED
04	307	¼ skein
310	3286	2 skeins
315	311	¼ skein
738	95	¼ skein

Backstitching Details

DETAIL	DMC THREAD	STRANDS
Corset lacing	738	2
Fangs	738	2

FOR THE COVEN

Know Your Power

Three little words imbued with ancient wisdom and the energy of witches throughout history. Know Your Power is a reminder we all need at times. In this design, the bold typography commands attention, reminding you to harness your power and embrace your unique abilities. The backdrop of delicate florals and leafy branches captures the essences of growth, renewal and transformation. The crescents symbolize the ever-changing nature of your power, which waxes and wanes like the phases of the moon. The intertwining of bold lettering and delicate blooms blends strength and beauty in a reflection your inner self.

Let your stitches weave a tapestry that reflects the magic within, and with each stitch infuse your own sorcery, creating a physical reminder that you are indeed a powerful creature.

Pattern details

FABRIC: 28ct Black Cashel Linen by Zweigart
COLORS: 6
STRANDS USED: 2
DIFFICULTY: Low
TOTAL STITCHES: 2,902

STITCH COUNT: 86w x 104h
FINISHED SIZE: on 28ct, stitched 2 over 2
FINISHED SIZE: on 14ct, stitched 2 over 1
WIDTH: 6.14in (15.5cm)
HEIGHT: 7.43in (19cm)

Thread

DMC THREAD	STITCHES	THREAD USED
35	198	⅛ skein
730	849	½ skein
733	1,017	¾ skein
734	173	⅛ skein
936	473	¼ skein
3803	192	⅛ skein

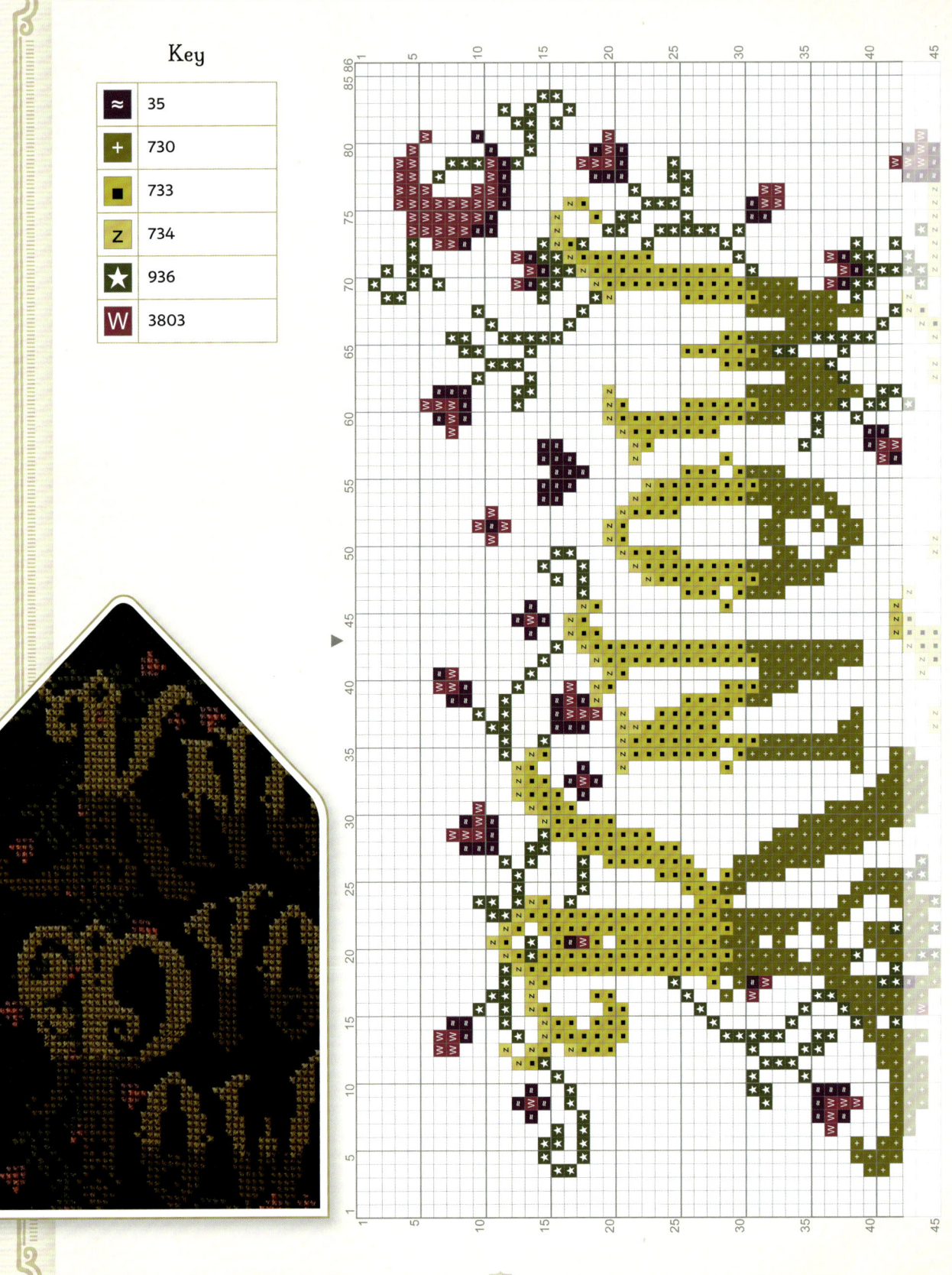

FOR THE COVEN

Three of Besoms

The word 'besom' is derived from the Old English 'besma', meaning 'a sweeping implement', or broom. They have been used for centuries to clean and purify spaces, sweep away negative energy and even protect homes from evil spirits! In many cultures they are believed to have magical properties and are used as divination and communication tools.

In Tarot, the Three of Wands represents the threshold of adventure and investing effort and emotion into your ideas and plans. Three is believed to be the perfect number – it is the number of harmony, wisdom and understanding, and of time: past, present, future; birth, life, death.

The three brooms stand tall and proud, reminding you to trust your abilities and set your sights on the path ahead with confidence, using the wisdom of experience to guide you through the present and into the future.

Pattern details

FABRIC: 28ct Grandpa's Sleeve Linen by xJuDesign
COLORS: 2
STRANDS USED: 2
DIFFICULTY: Low
TOTAL STITCHES: 1,550

STITCH COUNT: 64w x 94h
FINISHED SIZE: on 28ct, stitched 2 over 2
FINISHED SIZE: on 14ct, stitched 2 over 1
WIDTH: 4.57in (11.5cm)
HEIGHT: 6.71in (17cm)

Thread

DMC THREAD	STITCHES	THREAD USED
310	1,448	1 skein
611	102	⅛ skein

Backstitching Details

DETAIL	DMC THREAD	STRANDS
Besom ties	310	2
Besom twigs	310	1

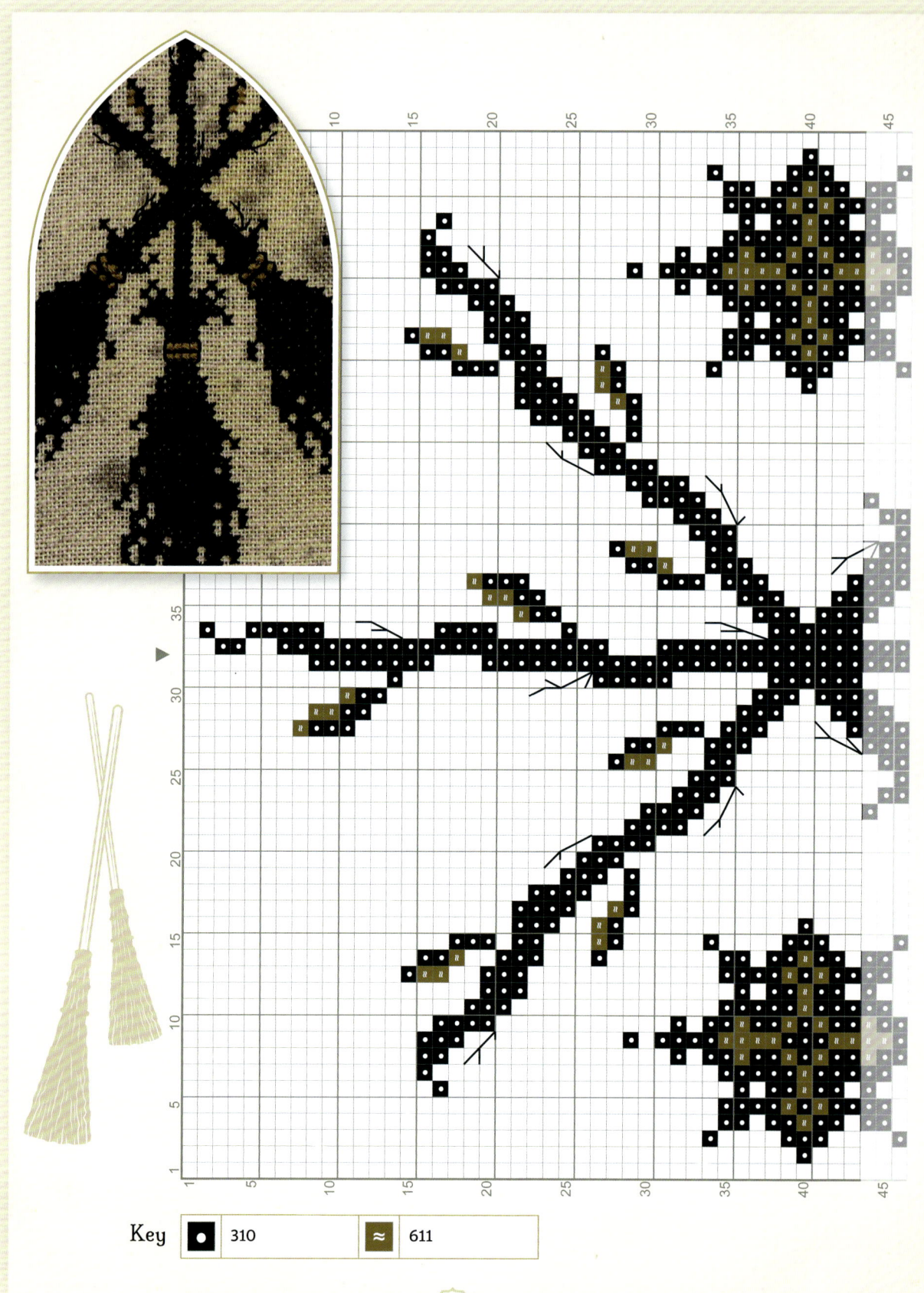

| Key | ● | 310 | ≈ | 611 |

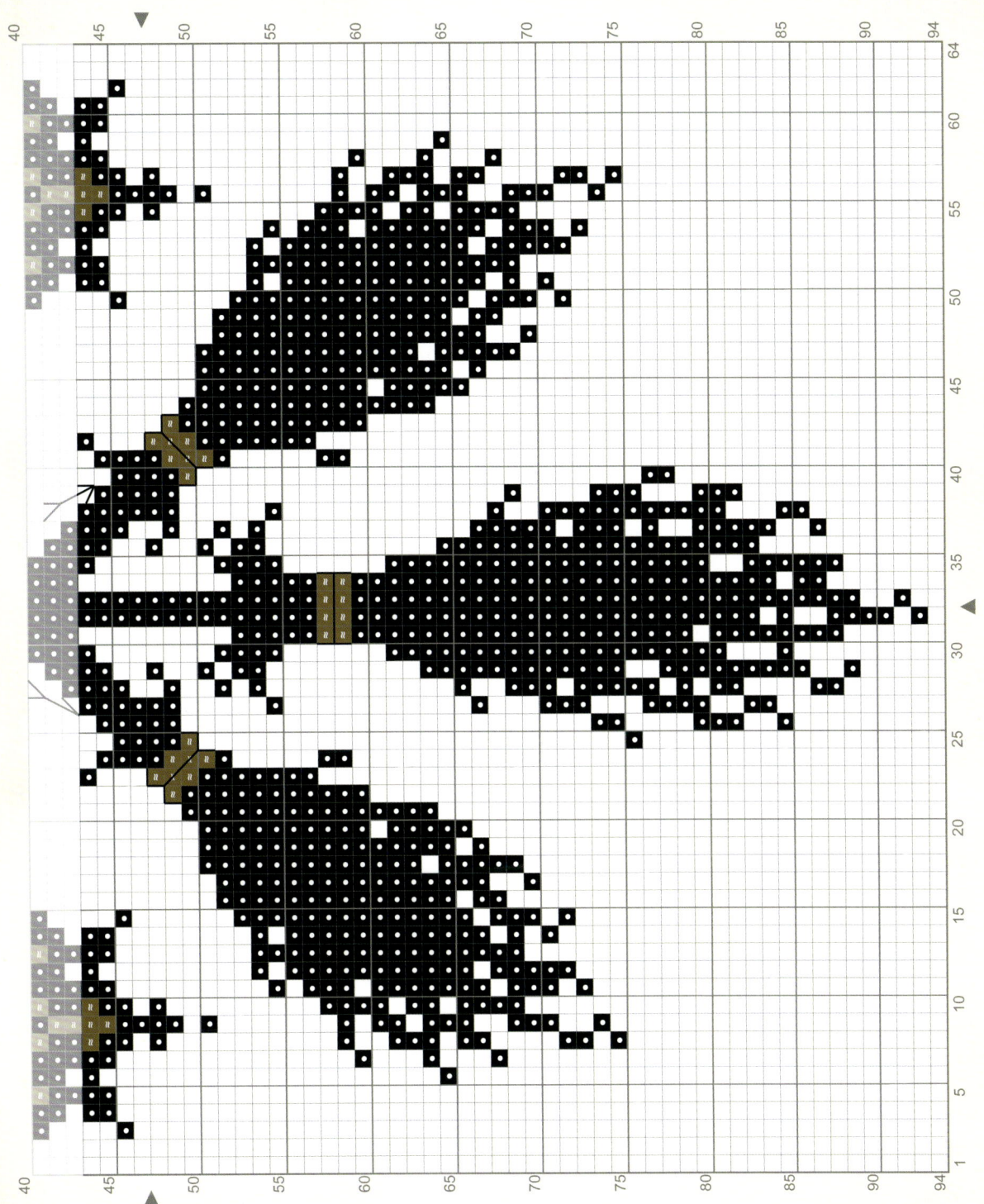

~ FOR THE COVEN ~

Witch's Cauldron

A companion piece to Three of Besoms. I believe that, sometimes, minimalism is more effective artistically than maximalism. I adore the simplicity of this design, which features imagery closely related to witchcraft. The moon phases represent change and transformation, the besoms purification, and the cauldron is the vessel for these actions.

Pattern details

FABRIC: 28ct Grandpa's Sleeve Linen by xJuDesign
COLORS: 2
STRANDS USED: 2
DIFFICULTY: Low
TOTAL STITCHES: 1,987

STITCH COUNT: 61w x 79h
FINISHED SIZE: on 28ct, stitched 2 over 2
WIDTH: 4.36in (11cm)
HEIGHT: 5.64in (14.5cm)
FINISHED SIZE: on 14ct, stitched 2 over 1

Thread

DMC THREAD	STITCHES	THREAD USED
310	1,955	1 skein
611	32	⅛ skein

Backstitching Details

DETAIL	DMC THREAD	STRANDS
Besom ties	310	2

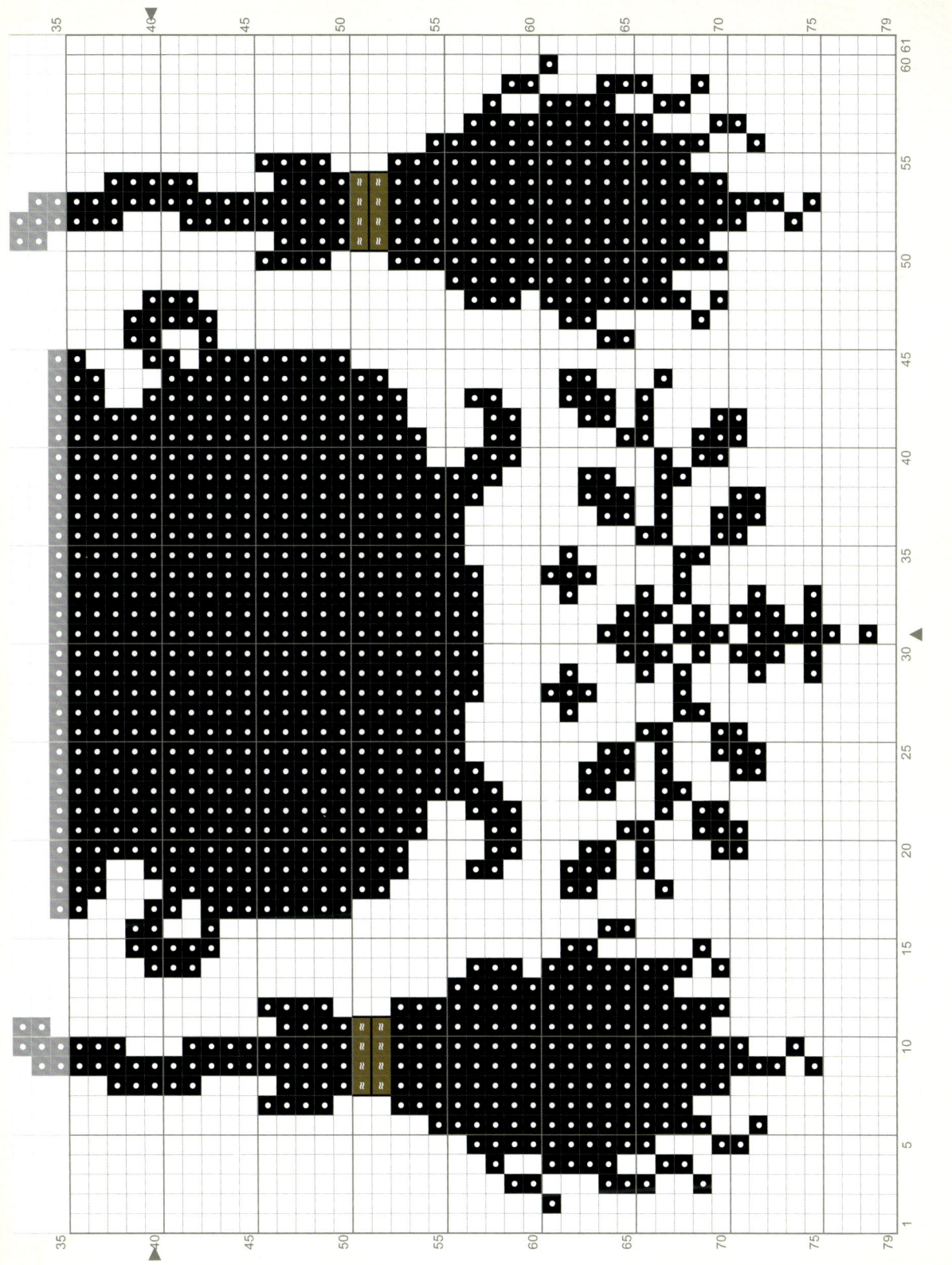

~ FOR THE COVEN ~

Superstitious Stitches

In a world full of uncertainty and unknowns, superstitions have long served as a way to seek comfort and control. From ancient times to the modern day, superstitions surrounding various items and symbols have persisted, passed down through generations as a way to ward off bad luck or invite good fortune.

However you integrate superstition into your life, or even if you don't, you have to admit it is wildly fascinating! This pattern features many symbols, from the ubiquitous black cat to skipping over cracks, each one a nod to the ancient folkloric beliefs.

In this design you will find 18 spooky symbols packed inside. Can you find them all? (If you are stumped, check the cheat sheet at the back of the grimoire on page 188.)

Pattern details

FABRIC: 32ct Anubis by Under the Sea Fabrics
COLORS: 2
STRANDS USED: 2
DIFFICULTY: Low
TOTAL STITCHES: 1,976

STITCH COUNT: 75w x 115h
FINISHED SIZE: on 32ct, stitched 2 over 2
WIDTH: 4.69in (12cm) HEIGHT: 7.19in (18.25cm)
FINISHED SIZE: on 14ct, stitched 2 over 1
WIDTH: 5.36in (13.6cm) HEIGHT: 8.21in (20.8cm)

Thread

DMC THREAD	STITCHES	THREAD USED
310	1,337	1 skein
3865	639	½ skein

Backstitching Details

DETAIL	DMC THREAD	STRANDS
Bird (beak and tail feather)	310	2
Bird cage	310	1
Cat (scaredy cat back hairs)	310	2
Coin (1 cent)	3865	2
Eyelashes	310	2
Hand	3865	2
Horseshoe (white stars)	3865	1
Mirror cracks	310	2
Rabbit foot	310	2
Spider	310	1
Spiderweb	310	1

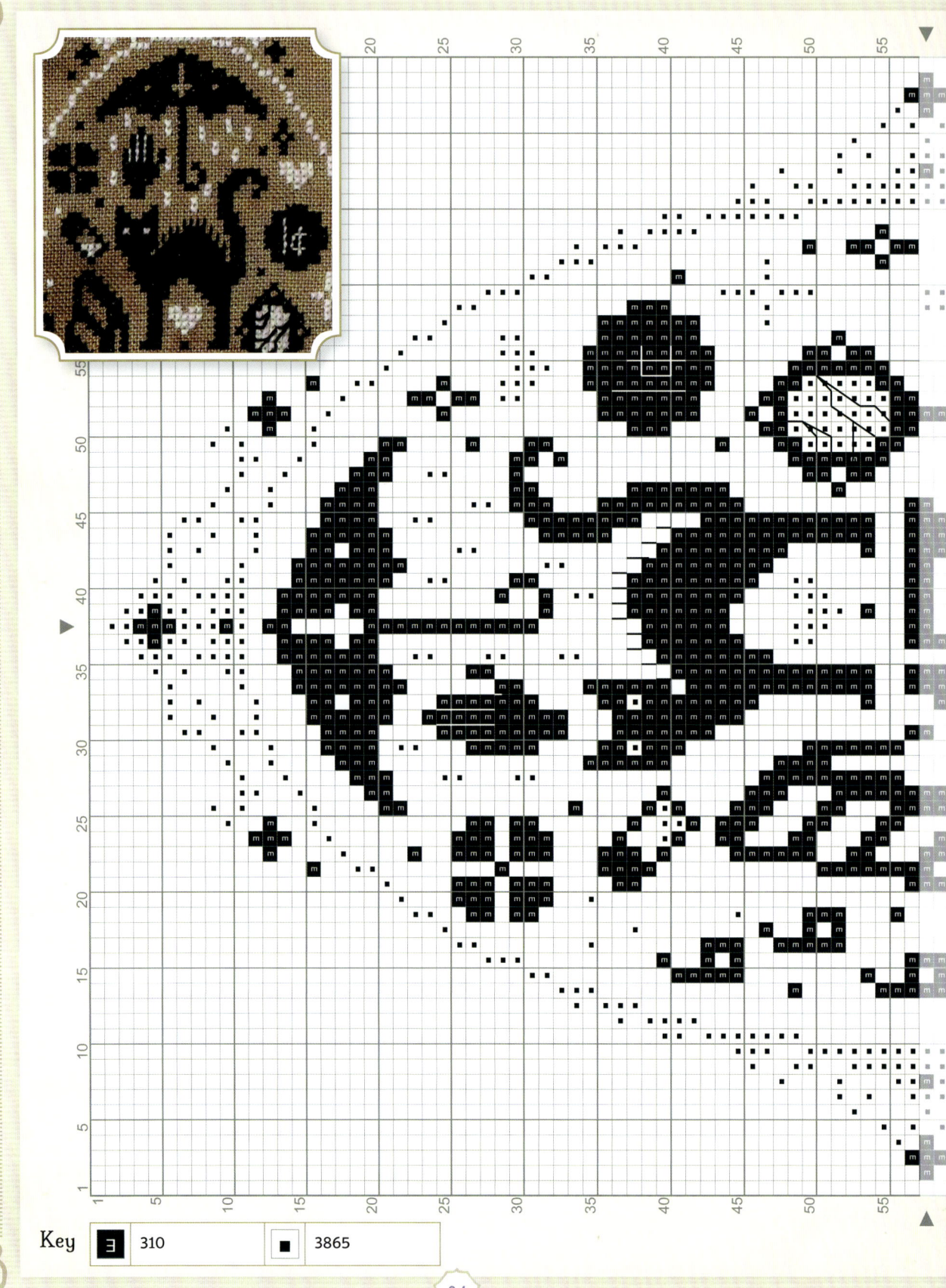

Key   ⴲ 310   ■ 3865

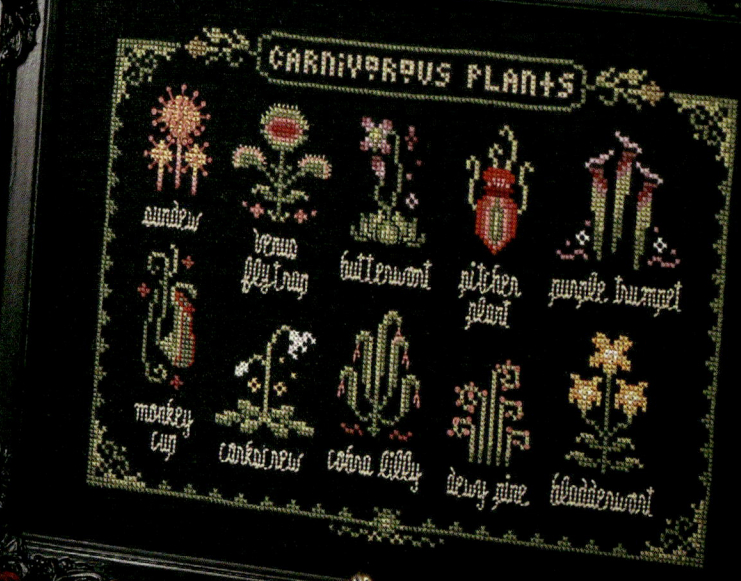

Gothic gallery

Haunted creations with a dash of whimsy

Embrace the allure of the gothic aesthetic as you bring these haunting designs to life. Inhabit a place where shadows dance, beauty meets darkness, and intrigue and mystery run amok. Drawing inspiration from the macabre romance of gothic literature, art and architecture is a cornerstone of my cross stitch designs. I am often inspired by vintage lace and filigree, and love to infuse its delicacy into many of my works. From hungry carnivorous plants to eerie iconic castles, this section has something that is sure to make your black heart skip a beat.

[2]

nd and then in England, where family lived from 1815 to 1820. 826 Edgar (who had secretly been engaged to Sarah Royster, a hbor's daughter) entered the versity of Virginia. He proved self a gifted student, with a special passion for literature. But unfortely, he was a less gifted card er: by the end of his first year he amassed debts of more than 0, along with a reputation for

In ear- tion bet- erupted i- later Edg- literary ca- He went t- ployment funds soon he enlisted name Edgar vember 1827 on Sullivan's He remained increasingly r- responding w- hope that his agree to purcha- army. At length part because Po- to enroll at We- because the last lan, who died in that they be reco-

Poe's appointm- ranged; he was to- cademy in July 1- me, after a few m- rmality in Richm- d relatives in Balt- ngthy stay with hi- ria Clemm, in whi- warmth and generos- ease his grief over death. More than tha- tivated by M- old d- becom-

dru- lan- Edg- scho- cove- enga- ents, h- their Poe's a- family inherita-

the same time, several of his new poems were accepted by magazines, tempting him once more to pursue his writing. But Poe still viewed enrolling at West Point as the only way to keep John Allan from cutting

Edgar A Poe

all financial support; so he report- to the Academy in July 1830. Any es for a future inheritance quick- ded, however. That October Allan remarried and made it that he did not consider Edgar a of his new family. An angry e shortly afterward led him to n his ward once and for all. n no further reason to stay at oint, Poe promptly got him- elled and left early in 1831 took up residence with h- in Baltimore and remained most of the next four y- ning his hand to short story w- ing to earn some desperat- mon- "M-

Ph- 1832 succ- but and li- S mo- it n- from from his e alm- P edit ems the nen diff Cle mo in cou to pla bin hea gui so spa sou sce mc the aw me Cl- roe sea hi- ts- h-

GOTHIC GALLERY

Coffin Case Bookmark

Mark your latest haunting read with every goth darkling's dream bookcase: these shelves are lined with curiosities, oddities, spell books, gothic literature and, of course, some friendly rats. Poe the rat is bravely teetering on the top, calculating his descent, while his mischievous pal Vincent is concocting a devilish plan to scare the wits out of Poe as he lands. Best friends scare together. Not sure how to make a bookmark? Check out the tutorial on page 38.

FUN WITCHY STITCHER FACT
Poe and Vincent were the names of my former pet rats, named after iconic gothic/horror masters Edgar Allan Poe and Vincent Price. They were delightful and sweet little babies, with so much personality. Rest in peace, my darling boys.

Pattern details

FABRIC: 14ct Grey Aida by Burlap Fabrics
COLORS: 13
STRANDS USED: 2
DIFFICULTY: Moderate
TOTAL STITCHES: 1,442

STITCH COUNT: 29w x 115h
FINISHED SIZE: on 14ct, stitched 2 over 1
WIDTH: 2.07in (5.25cm)
HEIGHT: 8.21in (21cm)

Thread

DMC THREAD	STITCHES	THREAD USED
03	36	⅛ skein
310	653	½ skein
321	26	⅛ skein
437	48	⅛ skein
498	74	⅛ skein
738	354	¼ skein
780	67	⅛ skein
782	32	⅛ skein
921	48	⅛ skein
3011	24	⅛ skein
3042	2	⅛ skein
3733	17	⅛ skein
3740	61	⅛ skein

Backstitching Details

DETAIL	DMC THREAD	STRANDS
Book details (dark)	310	2
Book details (light)	728	2
Candle flames	738	2
Picture frame and moth	310	2
Potion bottle sides	780	2
RIP banner details	310	2
Skull teeth	310	2
Skull vertebrae	738	2
Spiders	310	1
Tarot card	310	2

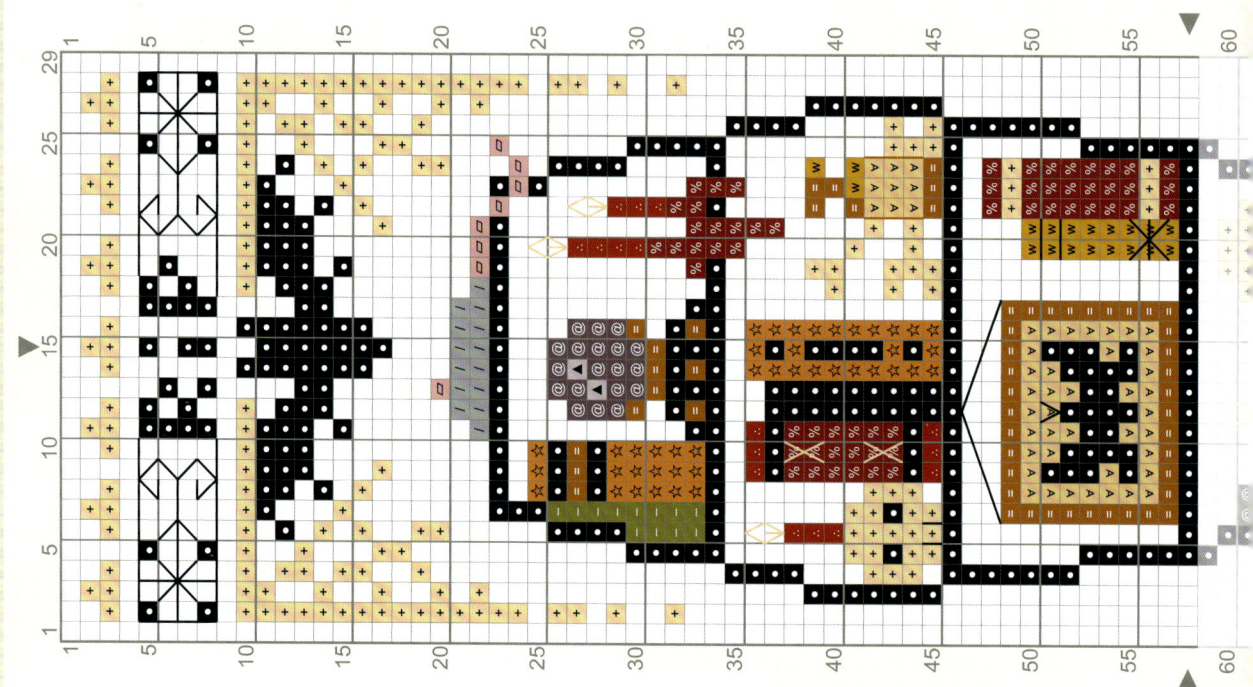

Key

/	03	+	738	▲	3042
●	310	=	780	▱	3733
∴	321	W	782	@	3740
∀	437	★	921		
%	498	—	3011		

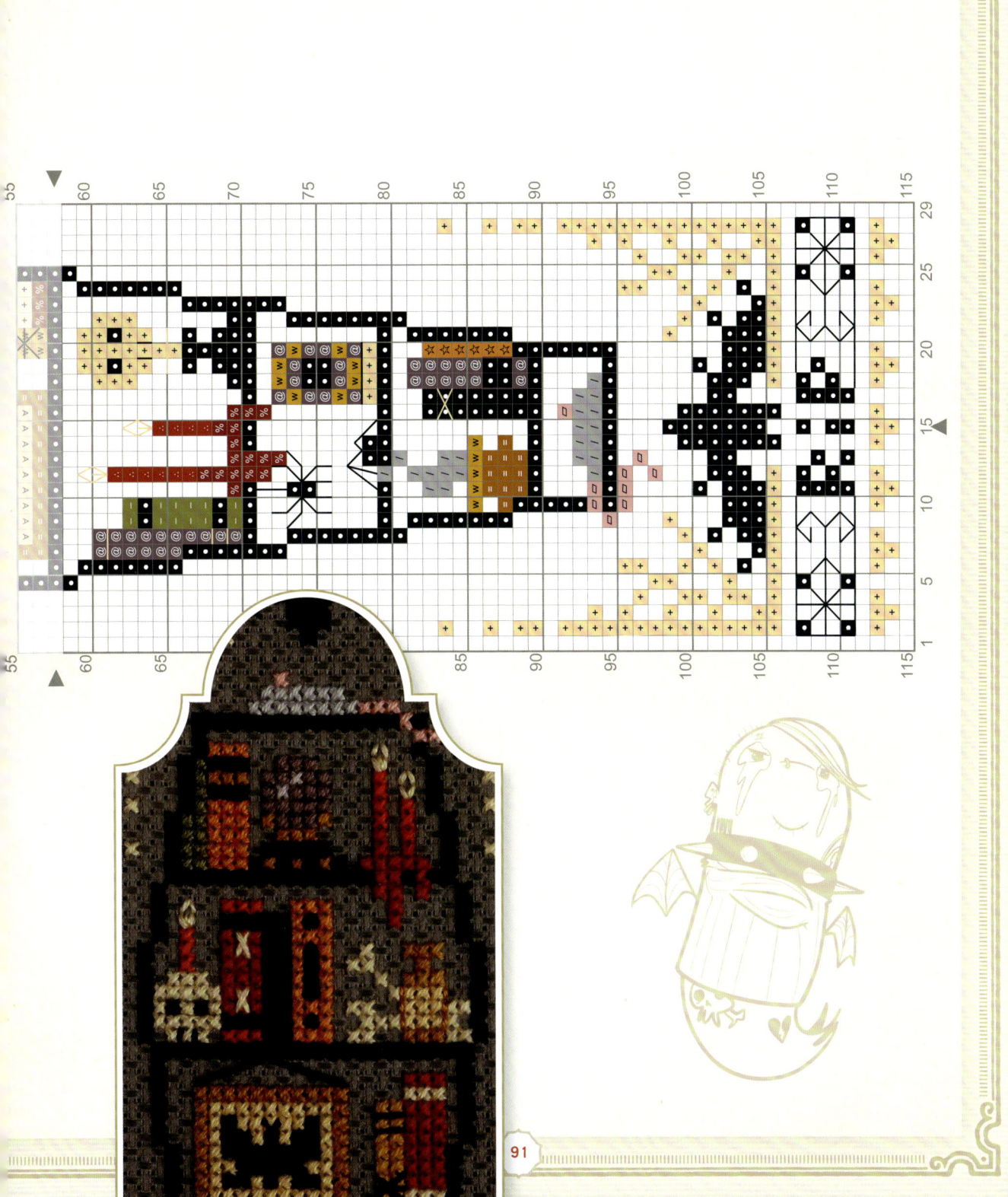

Memento Mori

Memento Mori is a Latin phrase that translates to 'remember you must die.' It reminds us of our mortality and the transitory nature of earthly pleasures. Remembering death is an ancient concept that encourages us to master our fear of it by recognizing the body's impermanence, and to nurture our immortal souls through the pursuit of knowledge.

This design uses iconic imagery often linked to the term 'Memento Mori'. The hourglass reminds us that our lifetime is limited, and the sand represents the passing of time, each grain counting a moment. The death's-head hawkmoth is often thought to be an omen of death and an adorable harbinger of doom.

I believe the term echoes another Latin phrase – 'Carpe Diem' (seize the day). It is about making each moment count – eat that cake, learn that new skill, go on that vacation – but with an added appreciation that your life is not guaranteed. What can I say? I am a glass-half-full kind of witch.

Pattern details

FABRIC: 28ct Morning Coffee Linen by xJuDesign
COLORS: 11
STRANDS USED: 2
DIFFICULTY: Low
TOTAL STITCHES: 3,679

STITCH COUNT: 69w x 110h
FINISHED SIZE: on 28ct, stitched 2 over 2
FINISHED SIZE: on 14ct, stitched 2 over 1
WIDTH: 4.93in (12.5cm)
HEIGHT: 7.86in (20cm)

Thread

DMC THREAD	STITCHES	THREAD USED
310	2,086	2 skeins
433	53	⅛ skein
610	174	⅛ skein
611	247	⅛ skein
612	101	⅛ skein
676	27	⅛ skein
780	323	⅛ skein
782	277	⅛ skein
783	333	⅛ skein
801	42	⅛ skein
869	16	⅛ skein

Backstitching Details

DETAIL	DMC THREAD	STRANDS
Skull mouth	310	2

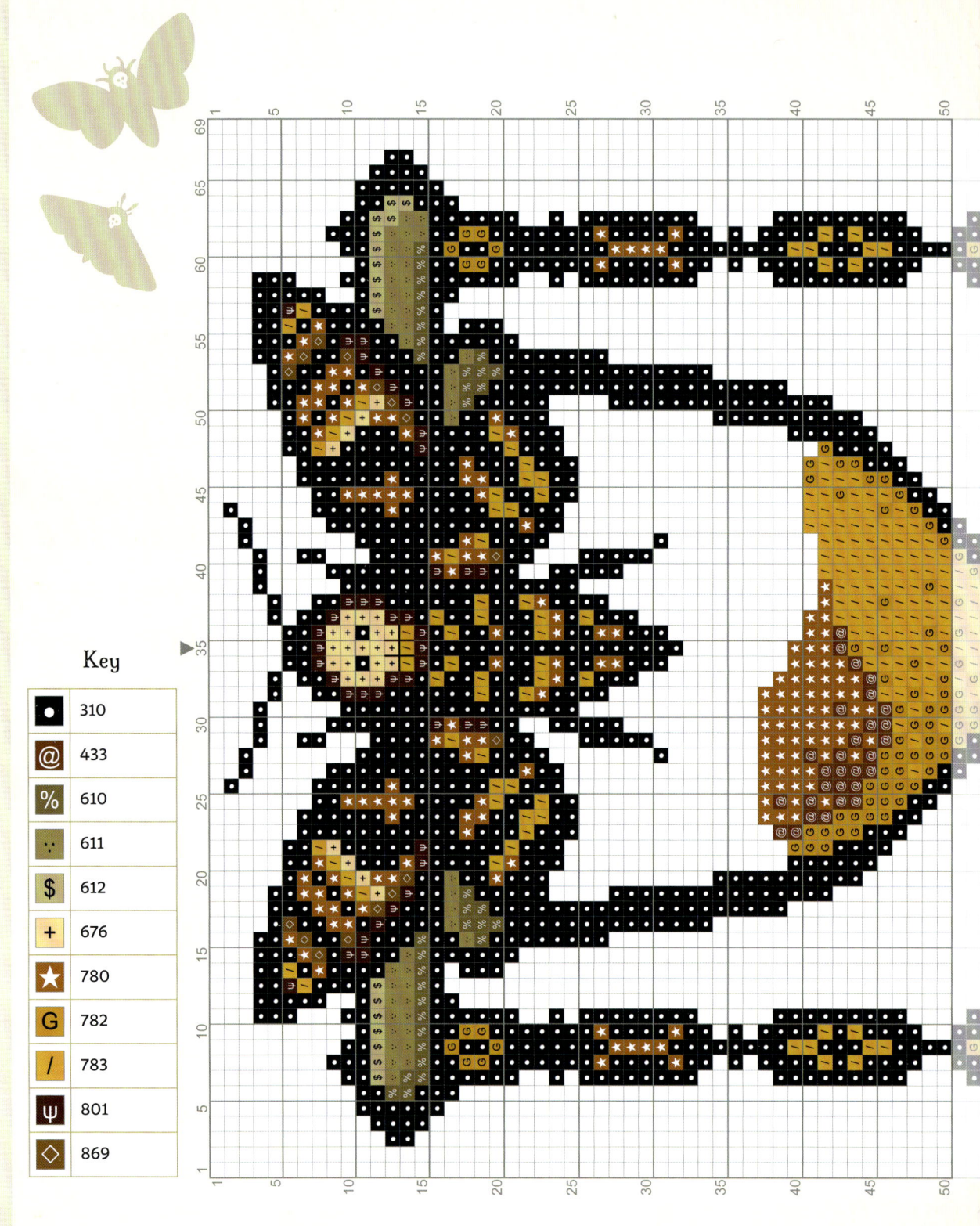

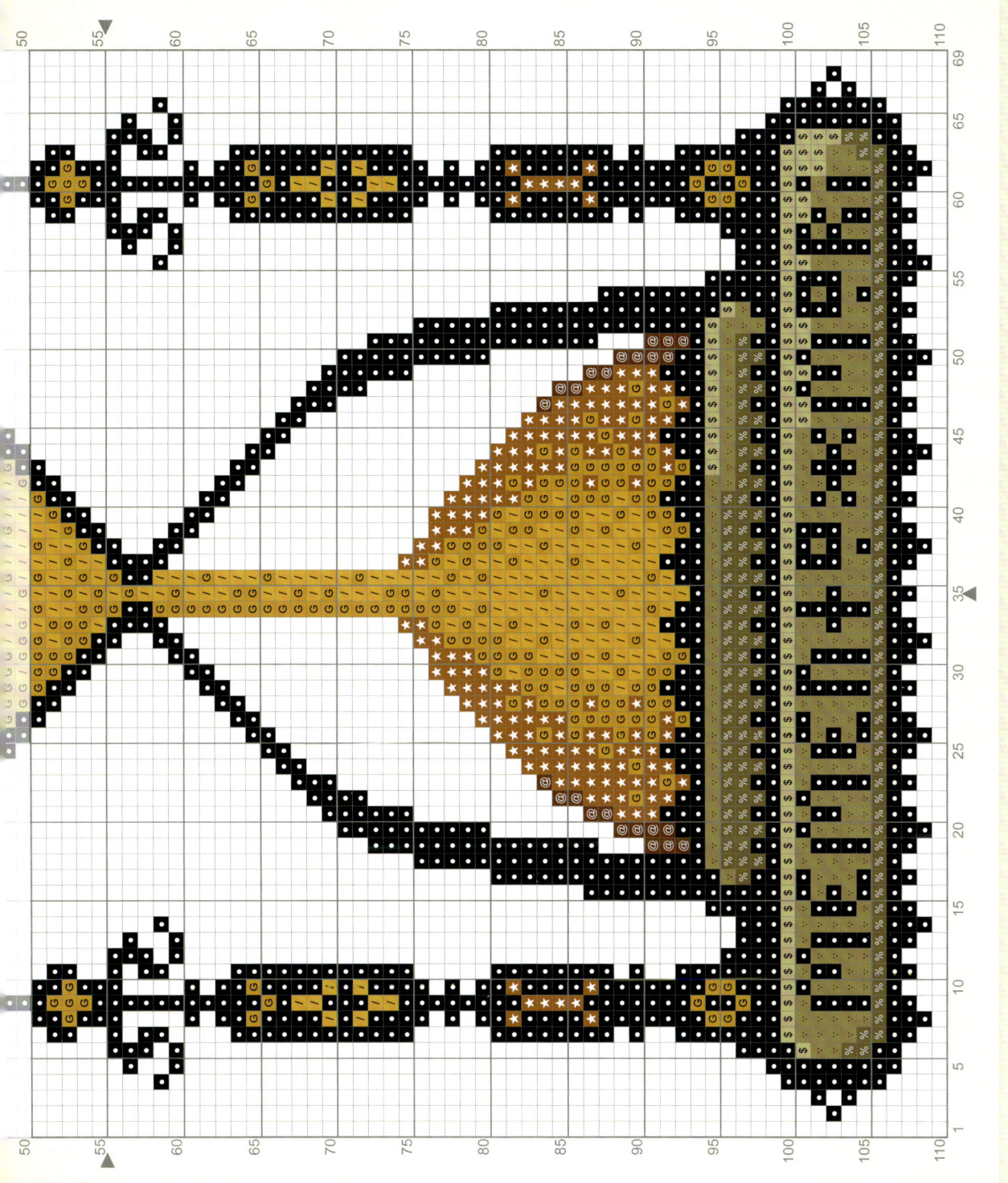

◦⁓ GOTHIC GALLERY ⁓◦

Victorian Haunt

If I can't live in my dream home, I will stitch it into existence. Victorian architecture has a death grip on my heart. Just picture it … sitting in the turret on a blissfully rainy day, candles flickering, a cross stitch in your lap and furry familiars peacefully sleeping in various nooks around the room. I'm pretty sure that is the definition of habitation paradise!

This pattern is the most difficult one out of all the offerings in this stitching grimoire. Subtle color changes and plenty of backstitch will give you more of a challenge. Do it for the ghosts!

Pattern details

FABRIC: 28ct Winter Wren Linen by Fox & Rabbit Designs
COLORS: 6
STRANDS USED: 2
DIFFICULTY: High
TOTAL STITCHES: 6,041

STITCH COUNT: 102w x 112h
FINISHED SIZE: on 28ct, stitched 2 over 2
FINISHED SIZE: on 14ct, stitched 2 over 1
WIDTH: 7.29in (18.5cm)
HEIGHT: 8in (20.5cm)

Thread

DMC THREAD	STITCHES	THREAD USED
02	229	⅛ skein
03	216	⅛ skein
04	226	⅛ skein
310	3,938	2 ½ skeins
E940 (GITD)	176	⅛ skein
3865	1256	¾ skein

Backstitching Details

DETAIL	DMC THREAD	STRANDS
Black elements	310	2
Cross-hatched windows	310	1
White elements	3865	2

Key

a	02
∴	03
=	04
●	310
★	E940
+	3865

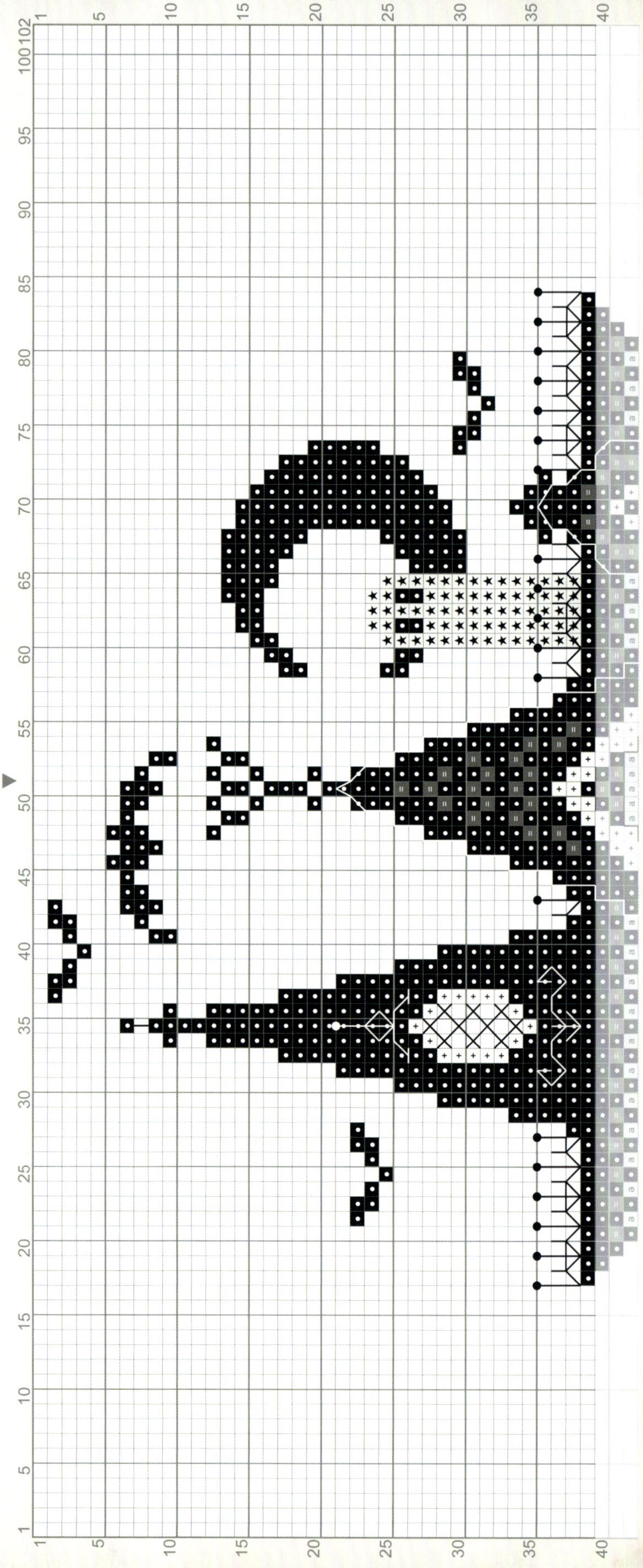

GOTHIC GALLERY

Nevermore

It's impossible to cover gothic unless we include the master of macabre himself, Edgar Allan Poe. Poe is dark and mysterious in both life and death, and is often referred to as the father of gothic literature.

This design is inspired by his beautiful and haunting work, 'The Raven'. The poem explores how grief can overcome a person's ability to live in the present and engage with society. It is centered around the narrator's journey into madness upon realizing that he will never forget his lost love. Poe uses the raven as a symbol of his struggle with loss.

The design features flowing calligraphy, on which perch three ravens. Why three? In numerology, three is linked to the past, present and future. Each raven represents the path to the narrator's inescapable fate, in spite of his efforts.

*'Take thy beak from out my heart,
and take thy form from off my door!'
Quoth the Raven 'Nevermore.'*
EDGAR ALLAN POE, 'THE RAVEN'

*'There is no exquisite beauty …
without some strangeness
in the proportion.'*
EDGAR ALLAN POE, 'LIGEIA'

Pattern details

FABRIC: 30ct Dark Spell Linen by The Primitive Hare
COLORS: 1
STRANDS USED: 2
DIFFICULTY: Moderate
TOTAL STITCHES: 4,379

STITCH COUNT: 174w x 80h
FINISHED SIZE: on 30ct, stitched 2 over 2
WIDTH: 11.6in (29.5cm) HEIGHT: 5.33in (13.5cm)
FINISHED SIZE: on 14ct, stitched 2 over 1
WIDTH: 12.43in (31.6cm) HEIGHT: 5.71in (14.5cm)

Thread

DMC THREAD	STITCHES	THREAD USED
310	4,379	3 skeins

Backstitching Details

DETAIL	DMC THREAD	STRANDS
Lettering details	310	2

Key

● 310

Gothic Gallery

Dracula's Castle

Where shadows linger and secrets whisper in the night. Bran Castle in Transylvania is famous for spawning the legend of Count Dracula, the most notorious of vampires. The fourteenth-century Romanian castle resembles Dracula's haunt as described in Bram Stoker's 1897 novel, in that both stand on rocky precipices and command spectacular views. However, Bram Stoker never visited Bran Castle or Transylvania, and the connection between the two is conjecture. Regardless of the true history, I enjoy imagining Bran Castle as Dracula's forever home.

When designing the pattern, I originally used a color palette that mirrored the real castle, but as I moved through the design process it became obvious that the macabre mansion was destined for a unique color scheme. Dripping with gothic vibes and blood-red thread, you can almost feel the heartbeat of the castle pulsing with dark energy and centuries-old secrets.

Not for the faint of heart, this crimson pattern will be a bit more arduous, thanks to its subtle color transitions. Stitchers beware before you sink your fangs into this one!

> *'Once again … welcome to my house.*
> *Come freely. Go safely; and leave*
> *something of the happiness you bring.'*
> BRAM STOKER, 'DRACULA'

Pattern details

FABRIC: 14ct Black Aida by Zweigart
COLORS: 6
STRANDS USED: 2
DIFFICULTY: High
TOTAL STITCHES: 5,347

STITCH COUNT: 120w x 100h
FINISHED SIZE: on 14ct, stitched 2 over 1
WIDTH: 8.57in (21.5cm)
HEIGHT: 7.14in (18cm)

Thread

DMC THREAD		STITCHES	THREAD USED
■	310	892	½ skein
■	814	1,014	1 skein
■	815	459	¼ skein
■	816	983	½ skein
■	817	1,549	1 skein
■	3801	450	¼ skein

Backstitching Details

DETAIL	DMC THREAD		STRANDS
Central window	■	310	2
C details lower	■	815	2
C details upper	■	817	2
D details lower	■	815	2
D details upper	■	817	2
Door	■	310	2
Roof above door	■	310	2

Key

●	310
+	814
$	815
→	816
⊗	817
▲	3801

~ GOTHIC GALLERY ~

Carnivorous Plants

Carnivorous plants are true carnivores that 'eat' all kinds of insects; large ones can even consume reptiles and small mammals. They grow in swampy areas and jungle that have little to no nutrition in the soil. Because of this, the carnivorous plant family has evolved to thrive by luring insects into their gruesome clutches to assist in their survival. These frightful florae can be found all over the world, and each species has a different appearance and method of luring their prey.

I have chosen a selection of ten hungry plant beauties, selected from the pantheon of carnivorous plans, from the majestic Venus flytrap (or 'Audrey' to classic horror fans) to its more obscure relatives. Each is unique in appearance, but all share a taste for flesh.

Carnivorous Plants is a much-requested companion piece to my 2022 Poisonous Plants pattern.

Pattern details

FABRIC: 28ct Black Cashel Linen by Zweigart
COLORS: 18
STRANDS USED: 2
DIFFICULTY: High
TOTAL STITCHES: 3,539

STITCH COUNT: 142w x 107h
FINISHED SIZE: on 28ct, stitched 2 over 2
FINISHED SIZE: on 14ct, stitched 2 over 1
WIDTH: 10.14in (25.75cm)
HEIGHT: 7.64in (18.75cm)

Thread

DMC THREAD	STITCHES	THREAD USED
310	27	⅛ skein
498	57	¼ skein
610	10	⅛ skein
611	16	⅛ skein
612	144	⅛ skein
613	561	¼ skein
712	34	⅛ skein
729	184	⅛ skein
814	25	⅛ skein
3012	699	½ skein
3051	1,357	1 skein
3687	170	⅛ skein
3688	11	1/8 skein
3803	99	⅛ skein
3834	27	⅛ skein
3835	58	⅛ skein
3836	33	⅛ skein
3853	27	⅛ skein

Backstitching Details

DETAIL	DMC THREAD	STRANDS
Butterwort base	310	2
Cobra lily	3687	2
Dewy pine	3687	2-strand French knot
Monkey cup	498	2
Plant names	613	1 (note French knot for letter 'I')
Pitcher plant	814	2
Sundew lines	3803	2
Sundew sticky balls	3687	2-strand French knot
Venus flytrap pink highlight	3687	2
Venus flytrap spikes	3012	2

Halloween

Pumpkins, ghosts and bats, oh my!

A collection of Halloween-inspired designs with a vintage feel. I wholeheartedly adore the style and character of vintage Halloween art; there is something so magical and special about its simplicity. Familiar motifs haunt these patterns, but I've given them a touch of Witchy Stitcher 'magic'. Have you ever wondered about the significance of iconic Halloween characters? Read on to learn a bit about the history of some of the imagery featured in this collection.

HALLOWEEN

Bats: medieval folklore depicted bats as witches' familiars. Seeing a bat on Halloween was considered to be quite an ominous sign. People also believed (and maybe still do) that if a bat were to fly into your house on Halloween night, then ghosts were present and had let the bats in.

Black cats: cats were worshipped long before they were demonized. The change came about through a mix of superstition and religious belief. It is said that Pope Innocent VIII declared black cats to be the 'Devil's favorite animal and idol of all witches'. People believed that witches would turn into black cats, or that these familiars were demon guides sent from below.

Ghosts: Samhain is an ancient Celtic festival that marks the end of the growing season, at around the beginning of November. It celebrates the dead, it is believed that the veil between the living and the dead as is especially thin at this time, allowing the spirits of the dead to visit the living.

Owls: owls are often associated with Halloween because, during the Middle Ages, owls were thought to be bad omens, or even witches. People also believed that if you heard an owl's call, someone was going to die. These nocturnal predators are highly active in October; they are hard at work establishing their winter territories and are often seen more frequently than during other months.

Pumpkins: the practice of carving and decorating jack-o'-lanterns originated in Ireland, although people originally used large turnips and potatoes. The name 'jack-o'-lantern' is derived from an Irish folk tale about a man called Stingy Jack. Stingy Jack is said to have tricked the devil into an inescapable situation. Irish immigrants brought the tradition to America, discovered pumpkins, and, as they say, the rest is history!

Skeletons/skulls: Historically, the festival of Samhain was linked with mortality because of the looming winter, and people believed that the ghosts of the dead and their rattling remains returned to earth.

◦ HALLOWEEN ◦

Vintage Halloween Bookmark

Under the glow of the turquoise Halloween moon a spooky little bat grins at your presence. 'Well, hello there fair cross stitcher. Can I interest you in snacks and the art of spooky craft?' If I were met with such a sweet creature of the night tempting me with such earthly delights, I would follow, no questions asked.

Mark your place in your spookiest Halloween book with this vintage-inspired bookmark. It's perfect for keeping your place in classic gothic literature or a pumpkin-laden recipe book.

Not sure how to make a bookmark? Check out the tutorial on page 38.

Pattern details

FABRIC: 14ct White Aida by Zweigart
COLORS: 8
STRANDS USED: 2
DIFFICULTY: Low
TOTAL STITCHES: 1,484

STITCH COUNT: 31w x 121h
FINISHED SIZE: on 14ct, stitched 2 over 1
WIDTH: 2.21in (5.5cm)
HEIGHT: 8.64in (22cm)

Thread

DMC THREAD	STITCHES	THREAD USED
310	485	¼ skein
C310	412	¼ skein
720	206	⅛ skein
722	31	⅛ skein
739	4	⅛ skein
783	19	⅛ skein
3847	85	⅛ skein
3849	242	⅛ skein

Backstitching Details

DETAIL	DMC THREAD	STRANDS
Bat nose	739	2
Bat teeth	310	2
Moon eyebrow	310	2

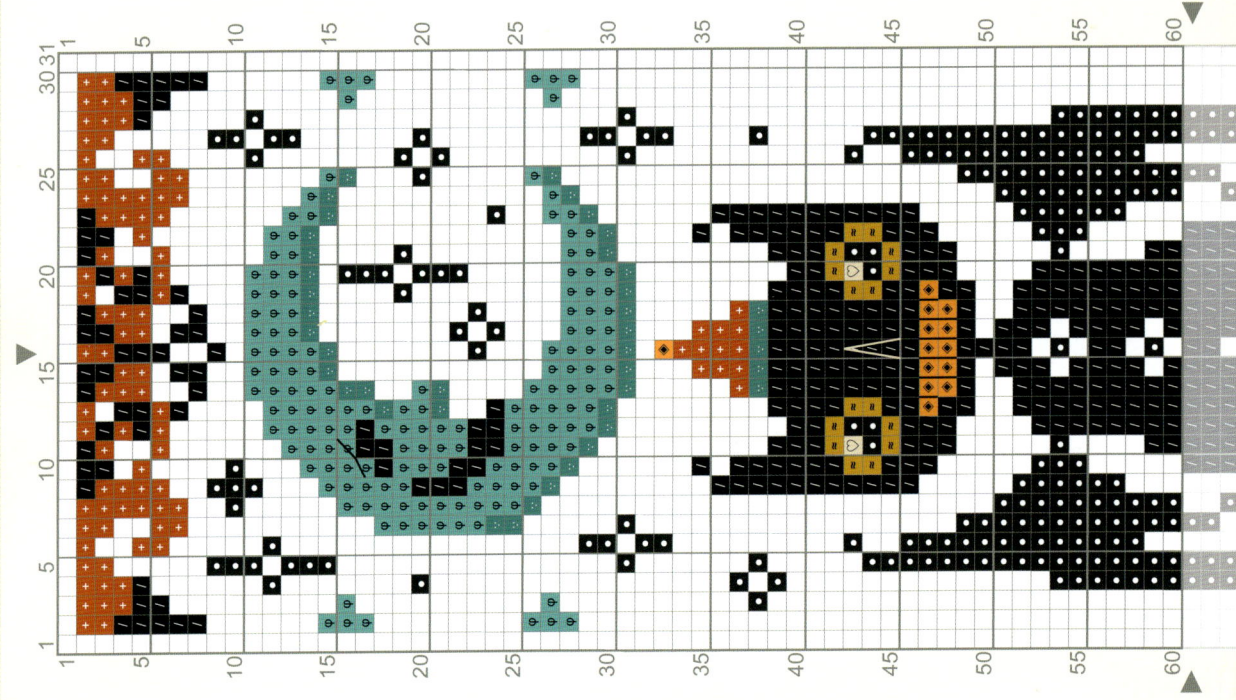

Key

/	310
●	C310
+	720
◆	722
♥	739
≈	783
■	3847
φ	3849

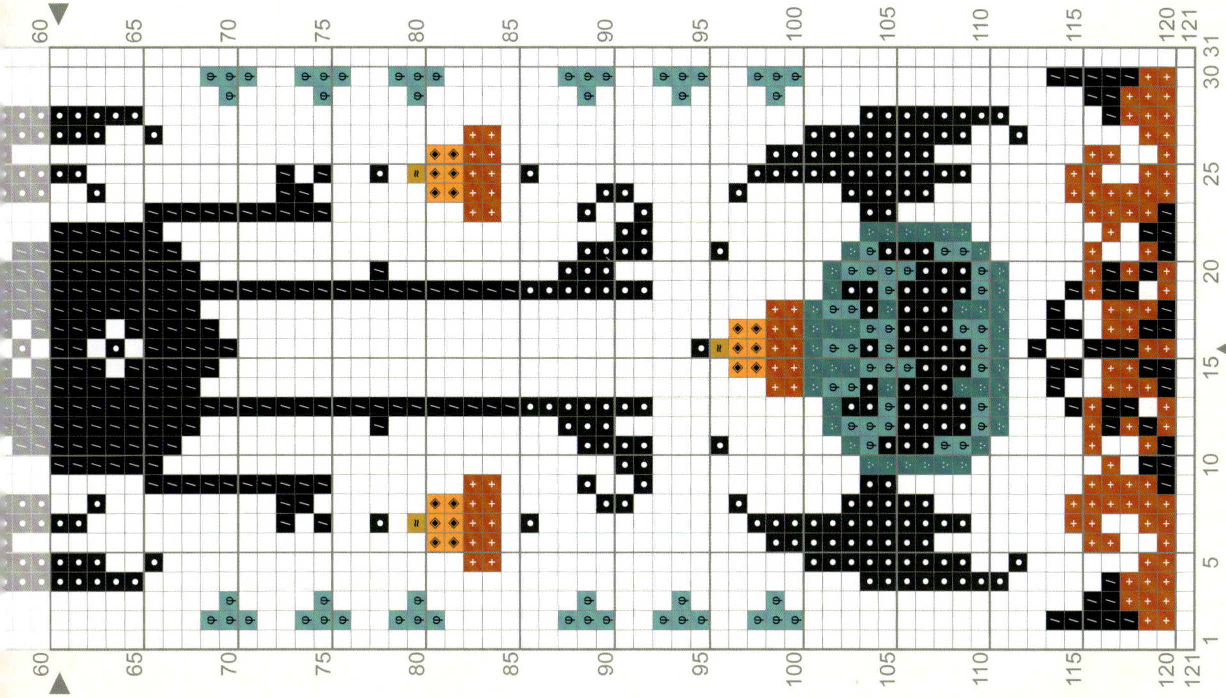

HALLOWEEN

Vintage Halloween Dolls

This haunting yet adorable trio is inspired by vintage folk-art papier-mâché dolls, and features classic Halloween characters: a skeleton, a ghost and a jack-o'-lantern!

This pattern makes me chuckle; it feels like there is a story to be told here. Perhaps the side-eyeing skeleton, the shocked and blushing ghost and the ecstatic jack-o'-lantern just witnessed a Halloween trick. If so, I think their expressions say a lot about their personalities. Stay away from Jack … he's trouble!

FUN WITCHY STITCHER FACT
This was the first piece I designed with a pattern book in mind. I actually made it in 2021, years before these words appear before you. This design holds a special place in my heart, and every time I look at it I am reminded of the vague dream I had, which has now come true.

Pattern details

FABRIC: 28ct Raw Cashel Linen by Zweigart
COLORS: 8
STRANDS USED: 2
DIFFICULTY: Moderate
TOTAL STITCHES: 4,108

STITCH COUNT: 86w x 101h
FINISHED SIZE: on 28ct, stitched 2 over 2
FINISHED SIZE: on 14ct, stitched 2 over 1
WIDTH: 6.14in (15.5cm)
HEIGHT: 7.21in (18.5cm)

Thread

DMC THREAD	STITCHES	THREAD USED
BLANC	17	⅛ skein
ECRU	532	¼ skein
310	2,302	2 skeins
720	252	⅛ skein
738	666	½ skein
740	311	⅛ skein
3340	8	⅛ skein
3824	20	⅛ skein

Backstitching Details

DETAIL	DMC THREAD	STRANDS
Party hat pompom	310	2
Skull doll eyes	310	2-strand French knot
Skull doll teeth	739	2
Skull teeth (smaller skull)	310	2
Spider on hat	BLANC	2

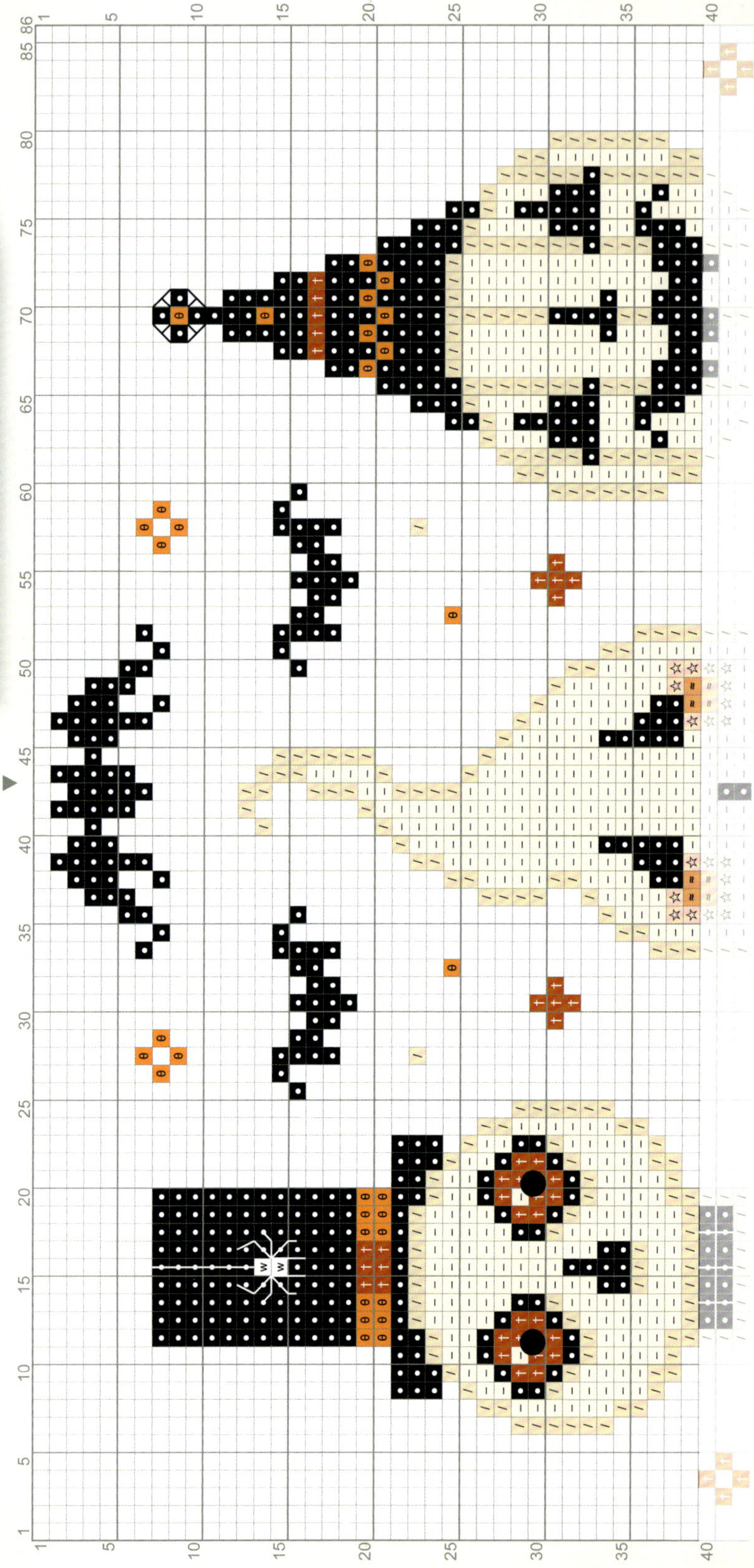

Key

W	BLANC
—	ECRU
●	310
†	720
/	738
θ	740
≈	3340
☆	3824

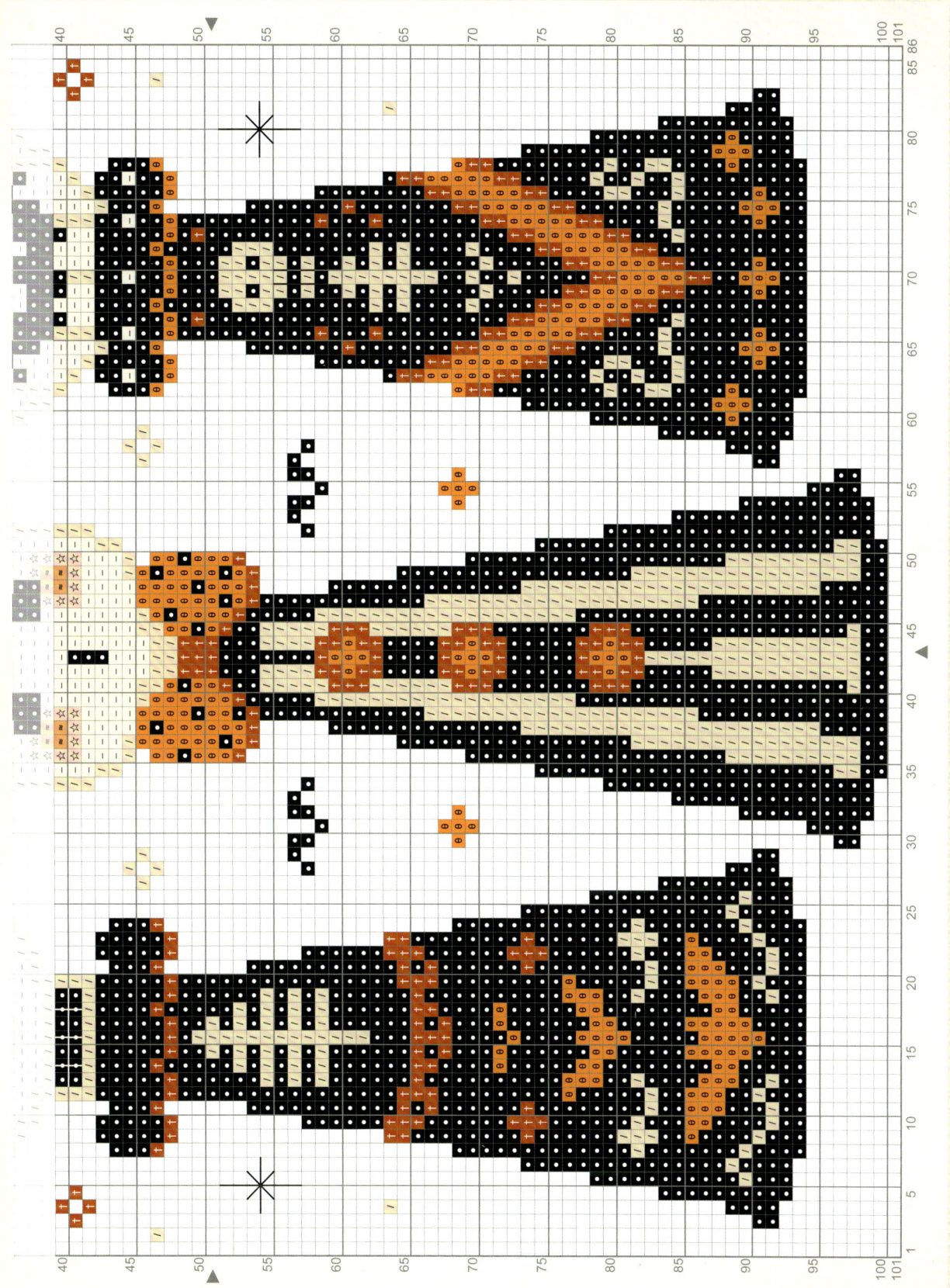

HALLOWEEN

Garden of Halloween

Cottagecore meets Halloween: equal parts spooky and whimsical! I imagine this pair living in an enchanted cottage nestled in a misty forest, the windows glowing with warm candlelight, and bright orange and red leaves lining a path to the door. Ghostly figures drift among the trees and the garden glistens in the moonlight. You can almost smell Halloween!

This beautiful autumnal couple are ready for a day at the human patch to pick their favorite of the season, dressed to impress at even the most casual of events.

Grab yourself a delicious cup of apple cider, light a pumpkin spice candle (I won't tell) and create a story for this delightful duo while you stitch them into existence.

'Every pumpkin deserves to shine.'
MARION MEISTER

PART ONE: Pattern details

FABRIC: 28ct Old Linen by xJuDesign
COLORS: 8
STRANDS USED: 2
DIFFICULTY: Moderate
TOTAL STITCHES: 3,384

STITCH COUNT: 67w x 115h
FINISHED SIZE: on 28ct, stitched 2 over 2
FINISHED SIZE: on 14ct, stitched 2 over 1
WIDTH: 4.79in (12cm)
HEIGHT: 8.21in (21cm)

Thread

DMC THREAD	STITCHES	THREAD USED
04	57	⅛ skein
310	1,865	1 skein
C310	522	¼ skein
720	270	⅛ skein
721	162	⅛ skein
738	332	⅛ skein
782	45	⅛ skein
919	131	⅛ skein

Backstitching Details

DETAIL	DMC THREAD	STRANDS
Arm detail/definition	04	2
Boot laces	C310	2
Eyelashes	310	2

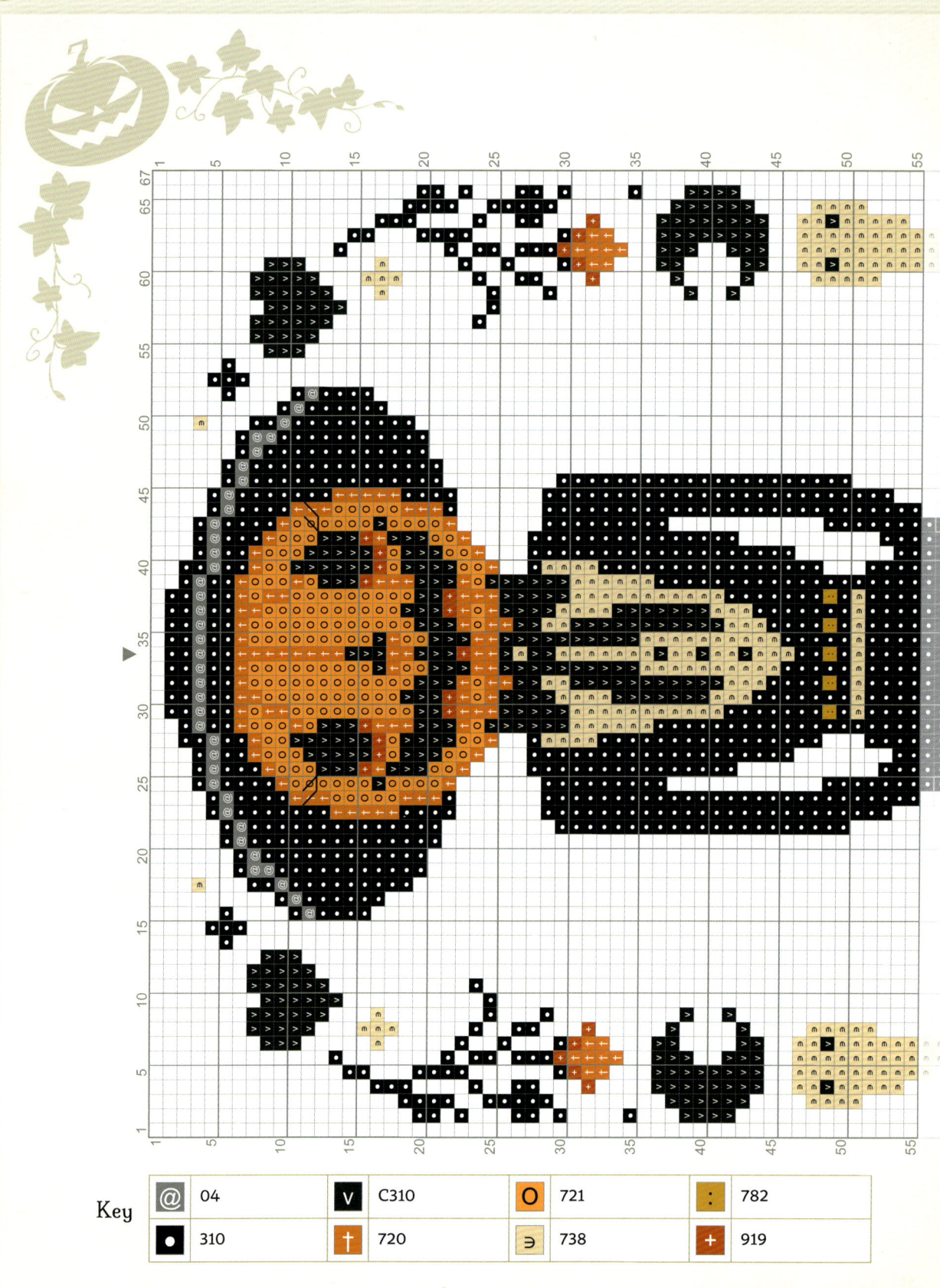

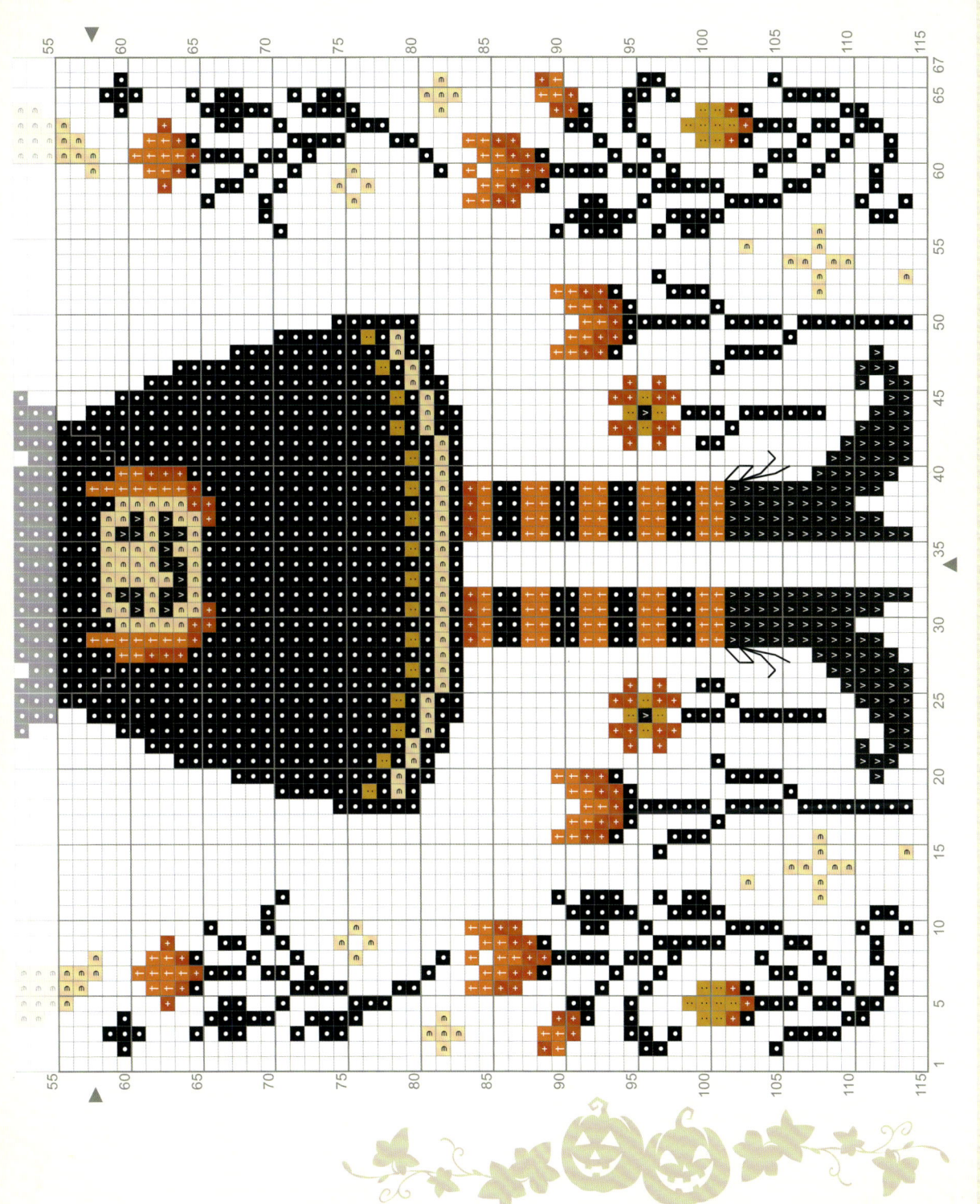

HALLOWEEN

PART TWO: Pattern details

FABRIC: 28ct Old Linen by xJuDesign
COLORS: 8
STRANDS USED: 2
DIFFICULTY: Moderate
TOTAL STITCHES: 3,144

STITCH COUNT: 67w x 115h
FINISHED SIZE: on 28ct, stitched 2 over 2
FINISHED SIZE: on 14ct, stitched 2 over 1
WIDTH: 4.79in (12cm)
HEIGHT: 8.21in (20.75cm)

Thread

DMC THREAD	STITCHES	THREAD USED
04	40	⅛ skein
310	1,844	1 skein
C310	478	¼ skein
720	149	⅛ skein
721	244	⅛ skein
738	274	⅛ skein
782	60	⅛ skein
919	55	⅛ skein

Backstitching Details

DETAIL	DMC THREAD	STRANDS
Arm detail	04	2

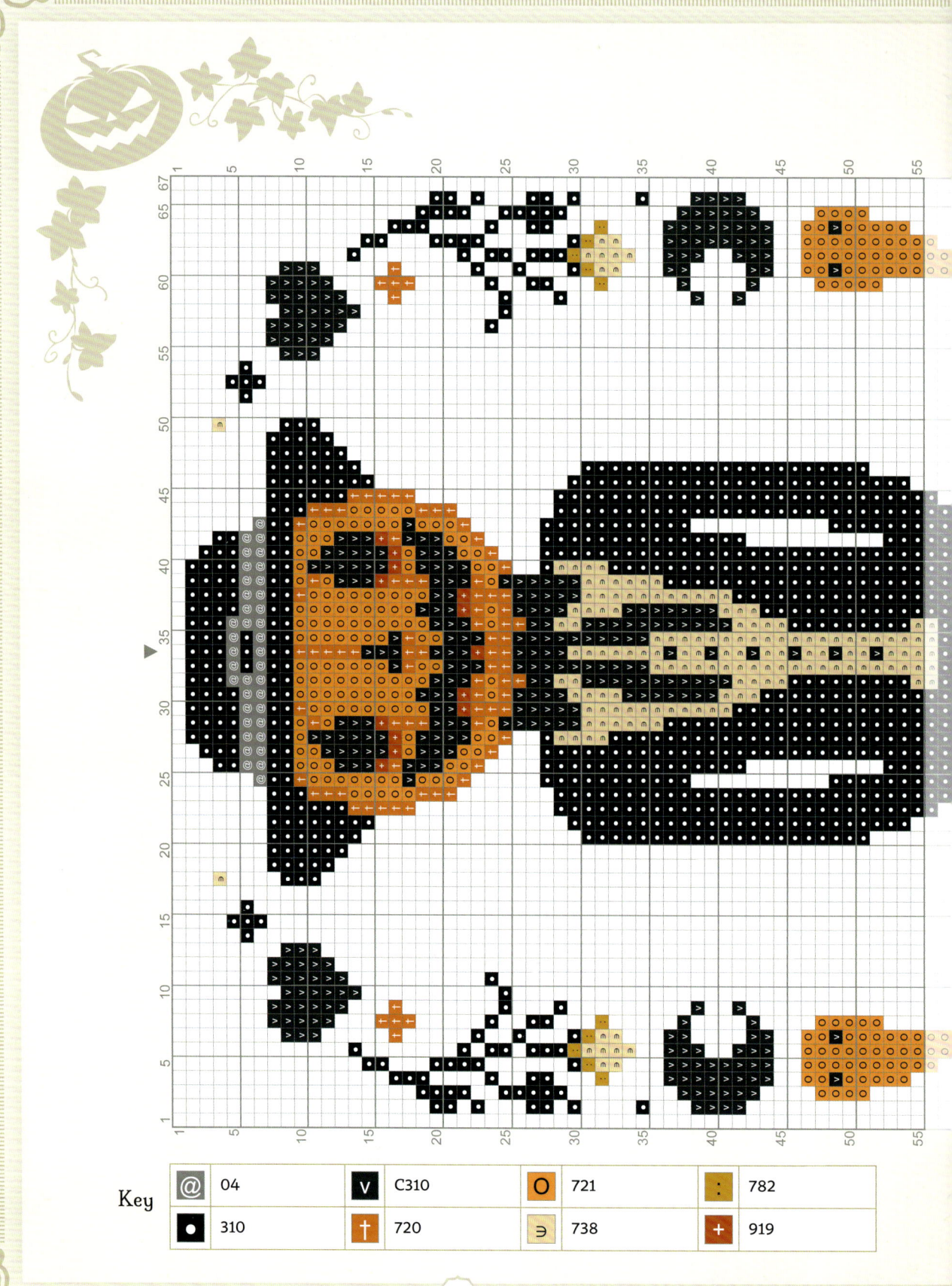

HALLOWEEN

Vintage Halloween Ferris Wheel

This pattern is an addition to my Vintage Halloween Fair Series, which features the Vintage Haunted Carousel and Vintage Halloween Fair, released in 2022 and 2023 respectively. The long-awaited and oft-requested Ferris wheel has joined the fair!

Step right up and take in the sights atop the 'EEK' Ferris wheel. Giggling ghosts run amok, cotton-candy-toting bats flap about, suspense-seeking skeletons roam and superstitious black cats hide in every corner. It's the sort of magic that sparks a nostalgia for the classic Halloween movies of childhood.

This ride would fit right in at Salem Haunted Happenings, the biggest Halloween event in the world, held in Salem, MA. Each year it draws over a half million visitors, and those are just the people. Imagine how many spirits there must be!

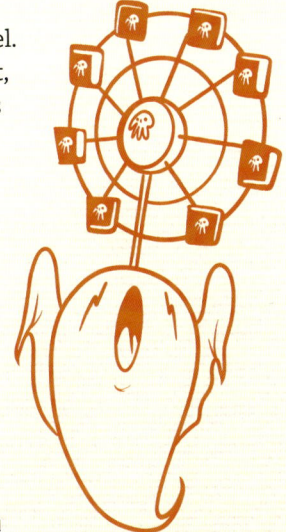

Pattern details

FABRIC: 14ct Grey Aida by Burlap Fabrics
COLORS: 11
STRANDS USED: 2
DIFFICULTY: Moderate
TOTAL STITCHES: 6,914

STITCH COUNT: 138w x 153h
FINISHED SIZE: on 14ct, stitched 2 over 1
WIDTH: 9.86in (25cm)
HEIGHT: 10.93in (27.75cm)

Thread

DMC THREAD	STITCHES	THREAD USED
04	182	⅛ skein
310	3,978	3 skeins
535	657	½ skein
613	444	½ skein
720	458	½ skein
740	333	¼ skein
741	44	⅛ skein
782	11	⅛ skein
839	8	⅛ skein
3848	673	½ skein
3849	126	⅛ skein

Backstitching Details

DETAIL	DMC THREAD	STRANDS
Flag	310	2
Kitten whiskers	310	2
Pumpkin stem	310	2
Skull teeth	310	2
Spiderwebs	310	2

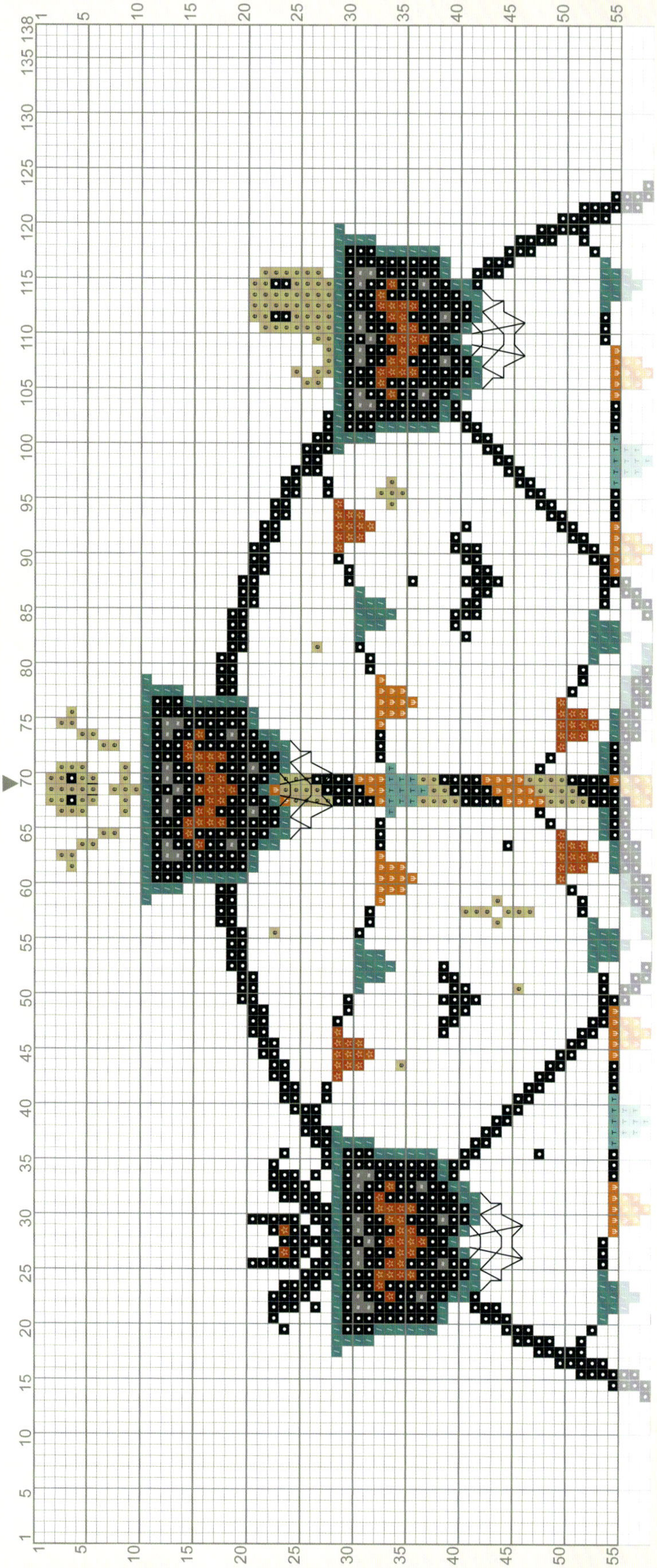

Key

≈	04
●	310
×	535
e	613
☆	720
Ψ	740
⊖	741
Y	782
♥	839
/	3848
T	3849

HALLOWEEN

Creepy Carnival

Come one, come all to the Creepy Carnival! The smell of cotton candy tickles your nose, the faint giggle of children can just be heard above the carnival music, and the 30-foot cat greets you with a mischievous grin. It's just another magical spooky night at The Witchy Stitcher's Creepy Carnival!

I adore the look and feel of vintage carnivals; there is such an innate creepiness to them. Capturing these elements can be quite difficult while keeping pattern size and stitch count manageable. This is one of my favorite challenges as a designer: doing just enough to give the vibe, without overdoing it.

Enjoy your stay at the carnival. Try the poisoned candy apples – they are frightfully delicious!

Pattern details

FABRIC: 28ct Raw Cashel Linen by Zweigart
COLORS: 11
STRANDS USED: 2
DIFFICULTY: Moderate
TOTAL STITCHES: 5,180

STITCH COUNT: 67w x 166h
FINISHED SIZE: on 28ct, stitched 2 over 2
FINISHED SIZE: on 14ct, stitched 2 over 1
WIDTH: 4.79in (12cm)
HEIGHT: 11.86in (30cm)

Thread

DMC THREAD	STITCHES	THREAD USED
ECRU	995	½ skein
310	2,110	2 skeins
C310	1,261	1 skein
420	61	⅛ skein
720	100	⅛ skein
C740	212	⅛ skein
900	118	⅛ skein
3828	144	⅛ skein
3847	12	⅛ skein
3848	123	⅛ skein
3849	44	⅛ skein

Backstitching Details

DETAIL	DMC THREAD	STRANDS
Bowtie	310	2
Kitty claws	310	2
Patch details	310	2
Stars	310	2
Ticket details	310	2

Key

ω	ECRU	@	900	
◆	310	s	3828	
X	C310	%	3847	
#	420	<	3848	
+	720	◐	3849	
∴	C740			

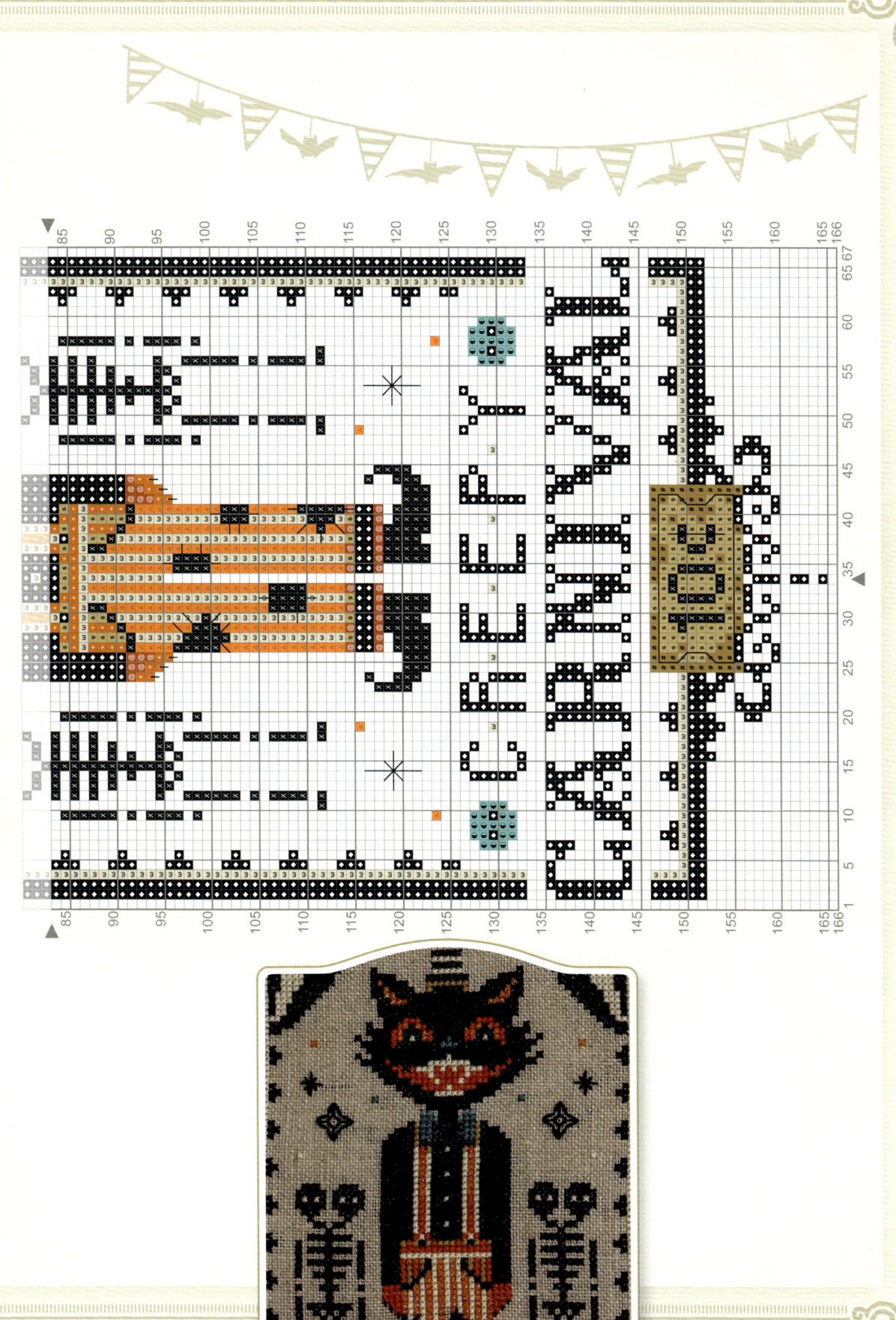

HALLOWEEN

Happy Owl-O-Ween

You may have noticed by now that I am not above a silly pun! Owl-o-Ween is haunting in full force with this sweet and swooping nocturnal darling – a whimsical wide-eyed owl perched upon a twisted tree branch, his eyes glowing and shimmering in the darkness. Perhaps he is pondering his next meal, or maybe world domination? Only the wise, feathered one knows …

This pattern is a perfect fit for a beautiful vintage oval frame like the one pictured. Oval patterns are not as common as the standard squares, rectangles and circles, and I feel like this spooky owl was just screeching for a more unique shape! I can confidently say that it is a hoot to stitch. I'll see myself out now.

Pattern details

FABRIC: 28ct Black Linen by Zweigart
COLORS: 8
STRANDS USED: 2
DIFFICULTY: Moderate
TOTAL STITCHES: 5,495

STITCH COUNT: 73w x 99h
FINISHED SIZE: on 28ct, stitched 2 over 2
FINISHED SIZE: on 14ct, stitched 2 over 1
WIDTH: 5.21in (13.25cm)
HEIGHT: 7.07in (18cm)

Thread

DMC THREAD	STITCHES	THREAD USED
ECRU	52	⅛ skein
310	2,338	2 skeins
C740	93	⅛ skein
900	2,866	2 skeins
3799	50	⅛ skein
3847	35	⅛ skein
3848	44	⅛ skein
3849	17	⅛ skein

Backstitching Details

DETAIL	DMC THREAD	STRANDS
Stars	310	1

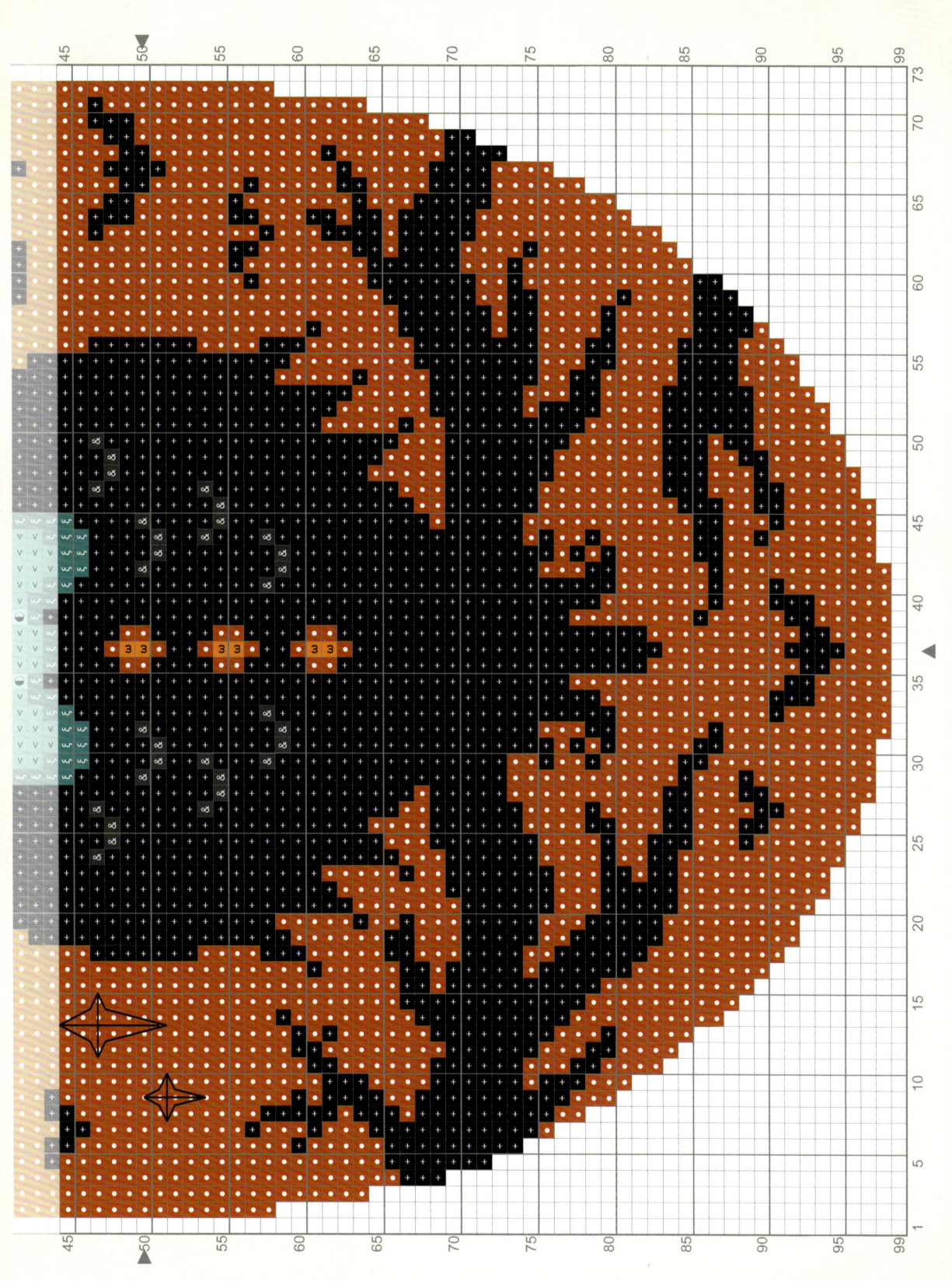

HALLOWEEN

Haunting Hour

When time stands still and ghosts roam free! When this clock strikes you had better grab that flashlight and pull those sheets up tight to your chin – the spirits are on the loose! This haunted grandfather clock screams vintage Halloween and makes my pumpkin heart twinkle. Simple but striking …

But beware! As you stitch this eerie design, time may seem to play tricks on you. The hours will slip silently away as you lose yourself in the autumnal oranges and antique whites. This project is sure to have you checking over your shoulder for spectral visitors.

Pattern details

FABRIC: 28ct Black Linen by Zweigart
COLORS: 8
STRANDS USED: 2
DIFFICULTY: Low
TOTAL STITCHES: 3,422

STITCH COUNT: 79w x 93h
FINISHED SIZE: on 28ct, stitched 2 over 2
FINISHED SIZE: on 14ct, stitched 2 over 1
WIDTH: 5.64in (14.5cm)
HEIGHT: 6.64in (17cm)

Thread

DMC THREAD	STITCHES	THREAD USED
310	1,435	1 skein
437	100	⅛ skein
720	115	⅛ skein
738	72	⅛ skein
739	298	⅛ skein
918	164	⅛ skein
920	819	½ skein
3799	419	¼ skein

Backstitching Details

DETAIL	DMC THREAD	STRANDS
Clock hand and knob	720	1 (including 1-strand French Knot)
Clock numbers	739	1
Stars	720	1

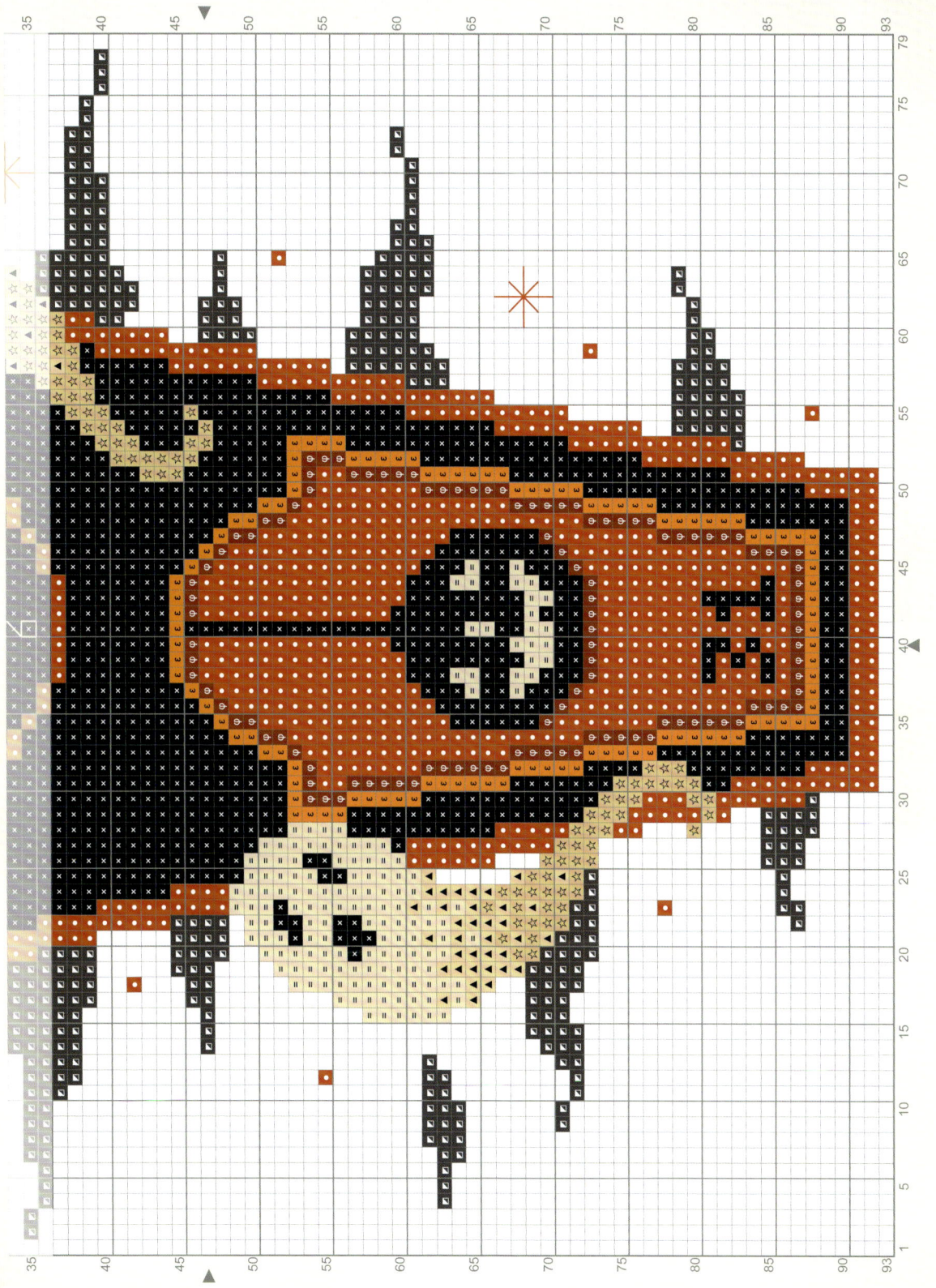

Haunted holidays

Holiday-inspired patterns with a creepy twist

Halloween enthusiasts around the globe are taking over traditional holidays (sorry not sorry). Us weirdos embody the spirit of All Hallows' Eve 365 days a year, and truly live the iconic words of Morticia Addams: 'Every day is Halloween.' Non-traditional twists on holidays bring me so much joy. The void outside the norm is my happy place. These haunted holiday designs are sure to spark conversation and bring a playful spooky vibe to your celebrations. Grab yourself some sweet treats and a spooky, cozy blanket, and embrace the magic of merging holidays!

~ HAUNTED HOLIDAYS ~

Merry Creepmas Bookmark

Why have Christmas when you could have Creepmas? Ever since Jack Skellington stole Christmas there has been a surge in spooky Christmas-inspired art and decor – a welcome addition to the holiday, in my humble witch opinion. Festive ghosts, twinkly lights and haunted wreaths? You had me at 'ghosts'.

Deck the halls with haunted spirits – 'tis the season to keep it spooky! Use this festive bookmark to keep your place in your dark Christmas tale. Not sure how to make a bookmark? Check out the tutorial on page 38.

FUN WITCHY STITCHER FACT
Ghosts are my favorite Halloween creepture! I collect ghost art, sculptures, mugs … you name it (although you may have guessed this already, based on how many ghosts I put in my patterns).

Pattern details

FABRIC: 14ct Black Aida by Zweigart
COLORS: 10
STRANDS USED: 2
DIFFICULTY: Low
TOTAL STITCHES: 1,155

STITCH COUNT: 33w x 113h
FINISHED SIZE: on 14ct, stitched 2 over 1
WIDTH: 2.36in (6cm)
HEIGHT: 8.07in (20.5cm)

Thread

DMC THREAD	STITCHES	THREAD USED
310	10	⅛ skein
433	18	⅛ skein
580	521	¼ skein
666	196	⅛ skein
739	177	⅛ skein
816	72	⅛ skein
3051	86	⅛ skein
3810	11	⅛ skein
3852	38	⅛ skein
3865	26	⅛ skein

Backstitching Details

DETAIL	DMC THREAD	STRANDS
Christmas tree light string	3051	2
Skull teeth	310	2

GingerDead House

HAUNTED HOLIDAYS

The snow glistens in the winter moonlight, the tree lights twinkle, towering candy canes tempt your taste buds ... and the GingerDead folk greet you? Welcome to a magical winter's night, conjured from the mind of The Witchy Stitcher. What I wouldn't give to call this creepy cookie casa my home! I imagine sitting by the crackling fire, watching the perfect snowflakes fall. The neighbors are interested yet cautious, and slow their pace as they stroll past. Does Krampus live here? An oddly festive witch? No matter who resides behind these doors, I am sure they have more than a few tricks up their sleeves.

In my own haunted abode, creepy Christmas decor is almost as ubiquitous as Halloween adornments – I have multiple themed trees, a seven-foot tall Jack Skellington door-greeter, skulls and taxidermy wearing Santa hats, and more lights than necessary. Bringing your personality and interests into the holidays is so much fun!

Pattern details

FABRIC: 28ct Selkie Linen by Under the Sea Fabrics
COLORS: 10
STRANDS USED: 2
DIFFICULTY: Moderate
TOTAL STITCHES: 5,497

STITCH COUNT: 91w x 120h
FINISHED SIZE: on 28ct, stitched 2 over 2
FINISHED SIZE: on 14ct, stitched 2 over 1
WIDTH: 6.5in (16.5cm)
HEIGHT: 8.57in (21.75cm)

Thread

DMC THREAD	STITCHES	THREAD USED
BLANC	12	⅛ skein
310	1,563	1 skein
321	110	⅛ skein
433	535	¼ skein
434	1,258	¾ skein
435	136	⅛ skein
436	191	⅛ skein
712	1,080	¾ skein
739	558	½ skein
921	54	⅛ skein

Backstitching Details

DETAIL	DMC THREAD	STRANDS
Santa hat	310	2
Skull teeth	310	2

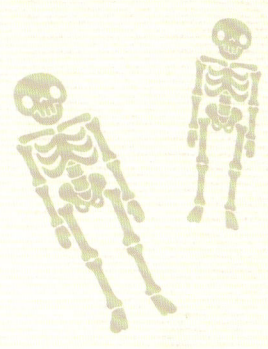

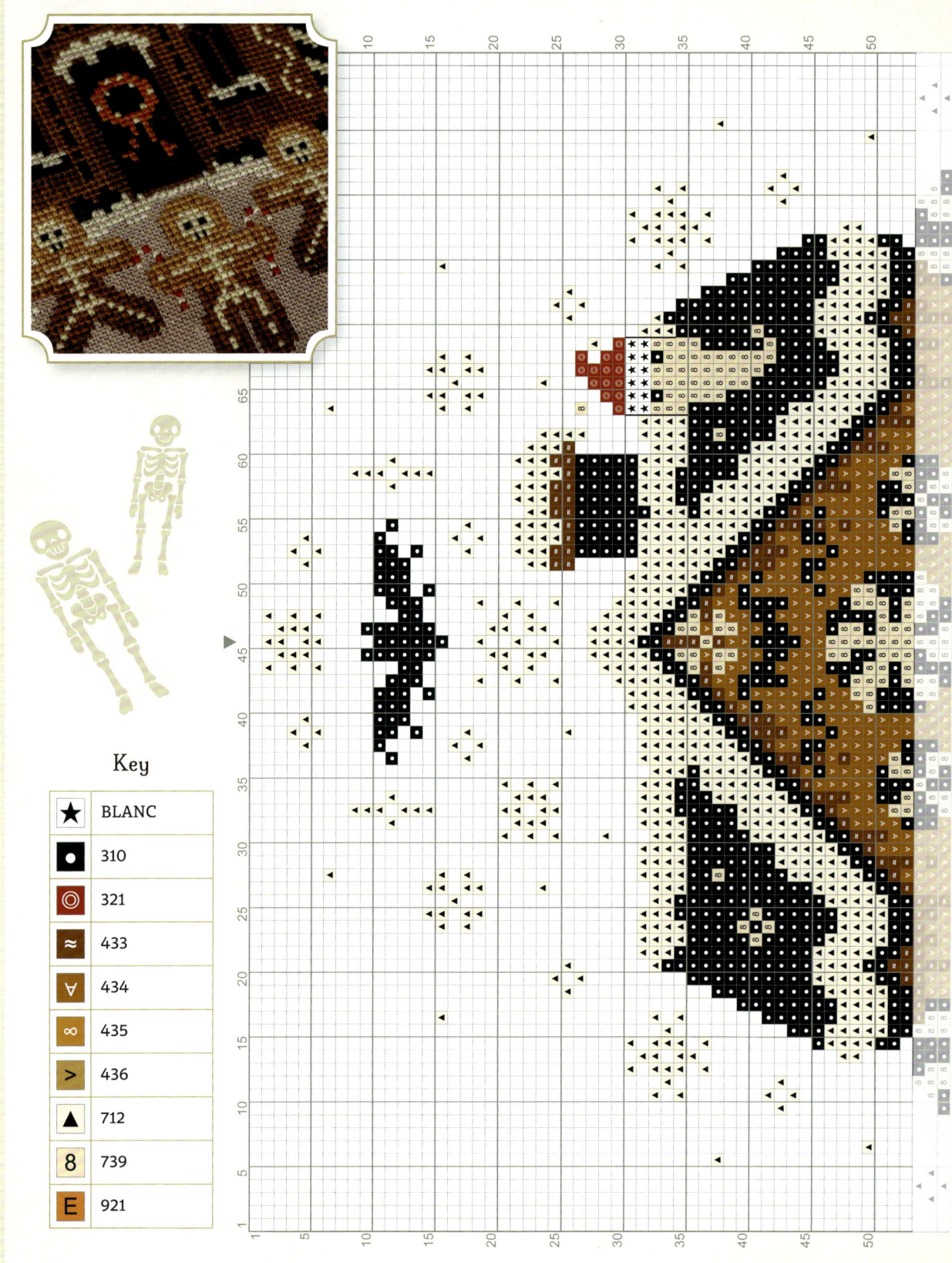

Key

★	BLANC
●	310
◎	321
≈	433
A	434
∞	435
>	436
▲	712
8	739
E	921

~ HAUNTED HOLIDAYS ~

Valloween Candy Corn Hearts

No, that isn't a typo! It is a mashup of Valentine's Day and Halloween that creates all kinds of spooky amours. For this design, I took the traditional candy hearts but gave them a candy corn color palette and a more rustic and primitive vibe – perfect for that spooky love in your life! I am sure even your cat would appreciate sitting on it.

FUN HALLOWEEN FACT
Did you know that candy corn used to be called 'Chicken Feed'? Though many would argue that candy corn tastes like chicken feed, that's not how it got its original name. This staple Halloween treat was created in the 1880s by George Renninger and sold to the masses by the Goelitz Confectionery Company (now known as Jelly Belly) at the turn of the century. Because corn was used to feed chickens, they called it 'Chicken Feed' and decorated the box with a colorful rooster.

Pattern details

FABRIC: 28ct Black Cashel Linen by Zweigart
COLORS: 4
STRANDS USED: 2
DIFFICULTY: Low
TOTAL STITCHES: 1,841

STITCH COUNT: 101w x 43h
FINISHED SIZE: on 28ct, stitched 2 over 2
FINISHED SIZE: on 14ct, stitched 2 over 1
WIDTH: 7.21in (18.25cm)
HEIGHT: 3.07in (7.75cm)

Thread

DMC THREAD	STITCHES	THREAD USED
310	232	⅛ skein
739	648	¼ skein
921	576	¼ skein
3852	385	¼ skein

—MINE

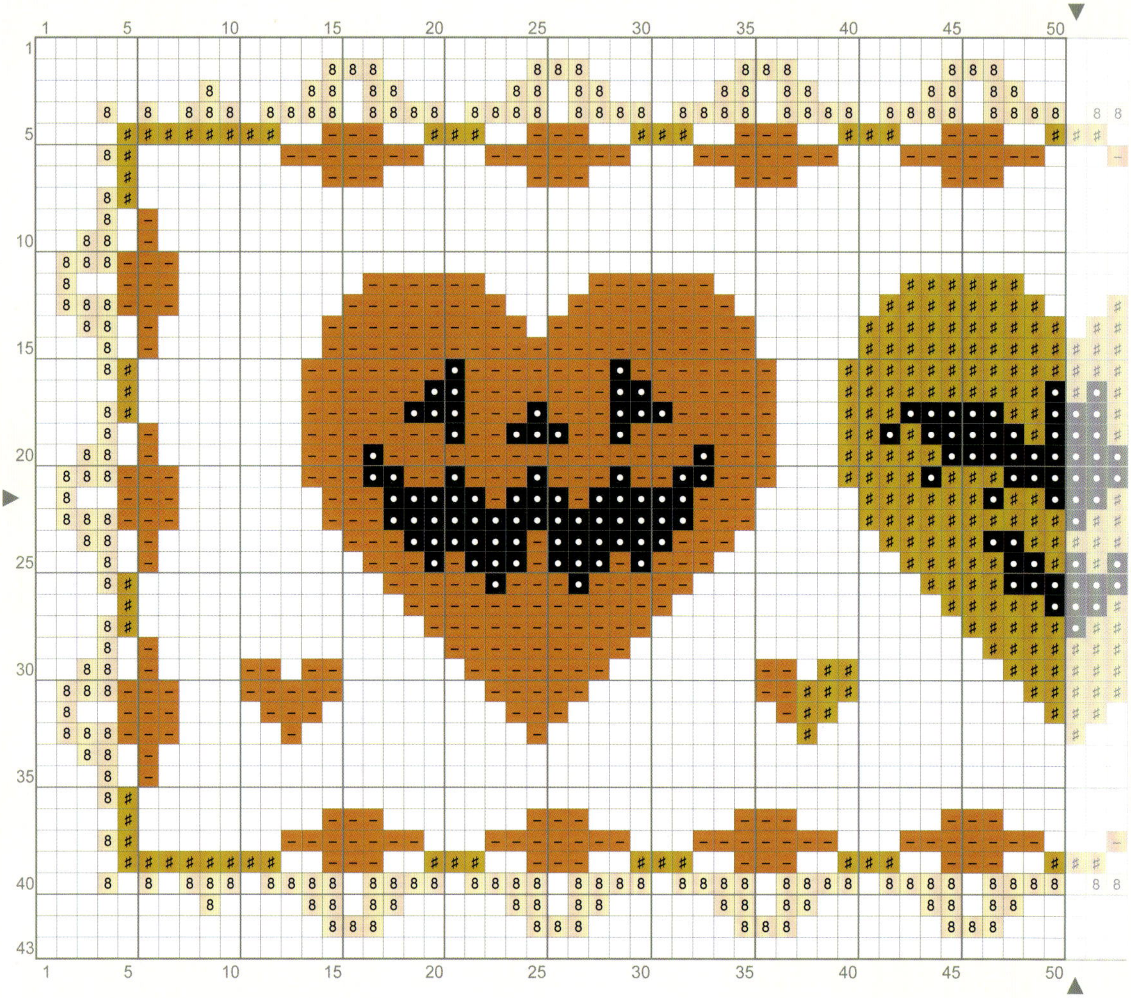

Key

●	310
8	739
—	921
#	3852

HAUNTED HOLIDAYS

Till Death

Celebrating Valloween? Gothic wedding in your future? Here is a lovely mix of devotion and spookiness! Till Death, or until the finality of death separates us on this earthly plane, is, in my opinion, the most romantic saying. To me, this doesn't mean love ends at death; it allows one to be free from grief upon parting because eternal love will reunite the separated souls in the afterlife.

This design features gothic typography in glow in the dark (GITD) thread, because love will guide you through the good and bad (light and dark) times. Each GITD skull atop the design represents one of a pair of bonded souls.

This would be the perfect gift for a newly joined couple, your partner, or even yourself. Loving yourself is hard work too.

Pattern details

FABRIC: 28ct Black Cashel Linen by Zweigart
COLORS: 6
STRANDS USED: 2
DIFFICULTY: Low (without beads)/ Moderate (with beads)
TOTAL STITCHES: 2,085

SEED BEADS: 74 (any black round seed bead will work. I used Mill Hill glass beads in color #02014). In place of beads, you can use DMC 310.
STITCH COUNT: 111w x 87h
FINISHED SIZE: on 28ct, stitched 2 over 2
FINISHED SIZE: on 14ct, stitched 2 over 1
WIDTH: 7.93in (20cm) **HEIGHT:** 6.21in (15.75cm)

Thread

DMC THREAD	STITCHES	THREAD USED
224	574	½ skein
309	76	⅛ skein
310*	74	⅛ skein
335	292	⅛ skein
E940 (GITD)	945	¾ skein
3733	124	⅛ skein

*if not using beads

Backstitching Details

DETAIL	DMC THREAD	STRANDS
Skull teeth	310	2

HAUNTED HOLIDAYS

Happy Easterween

Celebrate the duality of dark and light and tickle your black heart with a candy-coated Easterween delight!

Imagine a world where Easter egg hunts take place in haunted houses, pink bats soar under a candy corn moon and the fabled rabbit searches rows of gravestones for a fright! This is where you will find Easterween: Jack-faced eggs, bunny-eared skeletons and pastel pumpkin stacks adorn this haunted holiday design. As I am sure you can imagine, my home is very … black. Easterween gives me the perfect excuse to crack out the pale colors, shake up my haunt and confuse my resident ghosts!

Recommended extra supplies: chocolate mini eggs.

Pattern details

FABRIC: 14ct Black Aida by Zweigart
COLORS: 12
STRANDS USED: 2
DIFFICULTY: Low
TOTAL STITCHES: 3,219

STITCH COUNT: 83w x 125h
FINISHED SIZE: on 14ct, stitched 2 over 1
WIDTH: 5.93in (15cm)
HEIGHT: 8.93in (22.5cm)

Thread

DMC THREAD	STITCHES	THREAD USED
C310	339	¼ skein
470	247	⅛ skein
471	153	⅛ skein
722	106	⅛ skein
725	79	⅛ skein
900	25	⅛ skein
961	360	¼ skein
992	581	¼ skein
3326	6	⅛ skein
3814	497	¼ skein
3832	244	⅛ skein
3865	582	¼ skein

Backstitching Details

DETAIL	DMC THREAD	STRANDS
Floral vines	470	2
Skull eggs	C310	2

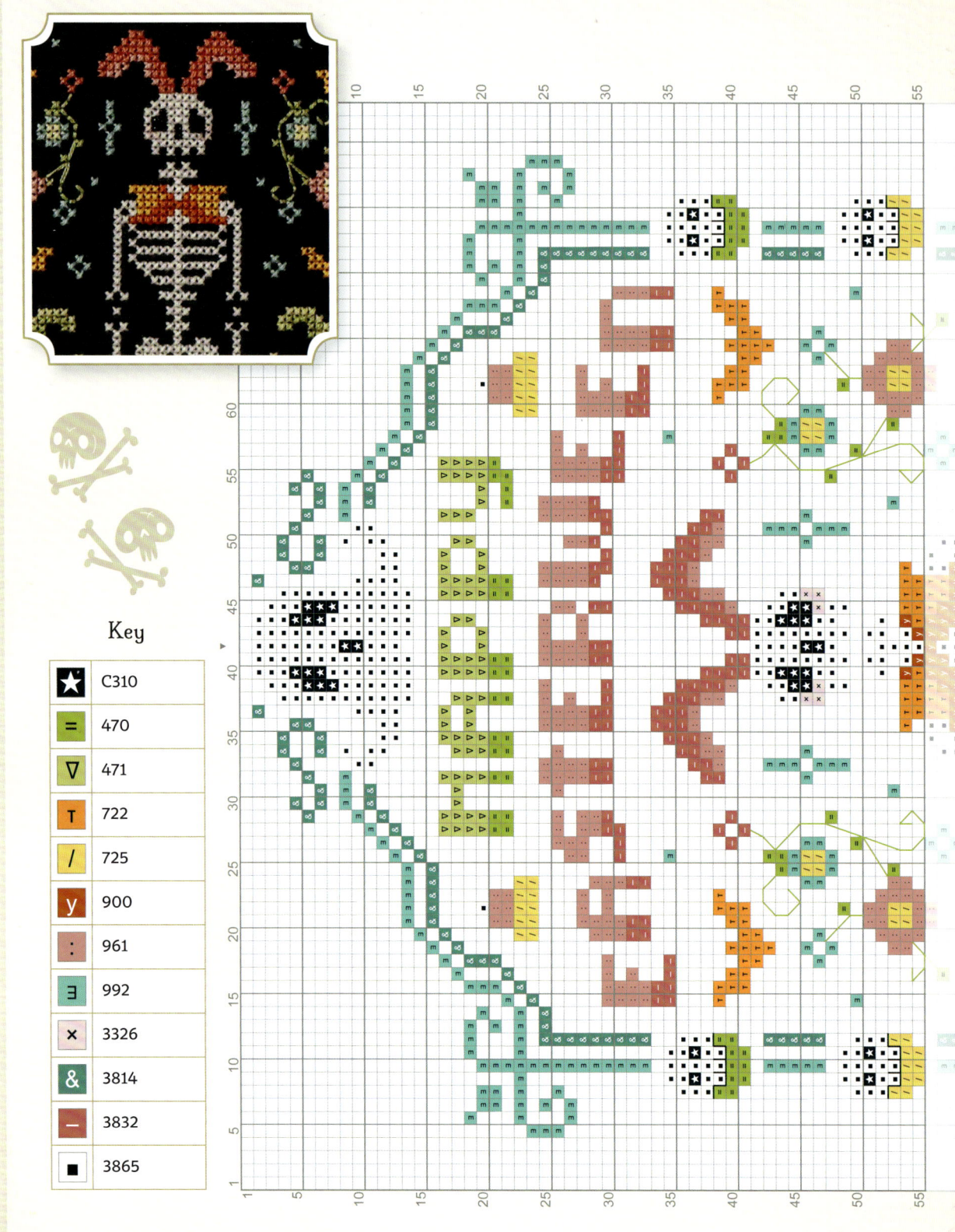

Key

★	C310
=	470
▽	471
T	722
/	725
y	900
:	961
∃	992
×	3326
&	3814
−	3832
■	3865

Finishing tips and tricks

OK, so you've stitched your project ... now what? It's time for finishing and framing! There are many ways to do this, but I am going to cover the two simplest and most common methods: in a standard picture frame and in an embroidery hoop. Both methods use techniques that are not permanent and can be easily undone, as they do not damage your work.

First, let's talk about washing your project. There is some debate about whether or not to do this, and I will fight for both sides as each situation is unique. When you stitch, the natural oils (and possibly snack dust) on your hands transfer to your fabric and, over time, will stain it, which is a good reason to give your project a little bath. That being said, if you are using hand-dyed thread or fabric, they may not be colorfast and you risk washing out your dyes and ruining the whole piece. Be sure to check with your supplier that your chosen canvas is colorfast. I only wash my projects if there is visible dirt and the fabric will not be damaged. I make good use of my grime guards and always wash my hands before stitching. A bonus to washing your project is that your stitches get a little puffed up, making them look fuller!

FINISHING TIPS AND TRICKS

How to wash and press your work

1 Prepare a lukewarm stitch bath with a couple drops of soap. Pre-rinse your project with cold water before submerging in the bubble bath.

2 Don't scrub the fabric, just swish it around. If you spot a stain, you can gently rub it (I sometimes use a soft-bristled toothbrush, brushing gently in a circular motion).

Materials needed
- ★ Your finished cross stitch
- ★ Mild soap (dish soap will do)
- ★ Lukewarm water
- ★ Bowl or sink
- ★ Two towels
- ★ Iron

3 Rinse with cool water a few times, making sure there are no more suds.

4 Roll up in a towel, giving a bit of pressure to get the excess water out, don't wring it!

5 Gently iron face down on a dry towel. Ironing on the reverse of your project with the towel underneath keeps your stitches from flattening out. Continue to iron until it is nice and flat, then leave to rest until it is fully dry.

How to frame in a hoop

Framing in a hoop is the easiest way to finish off your work of art. Wooden embroidery hoops are cheap and readily available at craft and thrift stores. You can paint or customize them to match your haunt, too! I painted this hoop (page 185) black with acrylic paint and sealed it with a glossy varnish.

1 Trace the outside edge of the inner hoop on piece of felt (if adding backing), then cut out. This will cover the back of your project.

2 Lay your stitch over the inner hoop, centering it as best as you can, then place the outer hoop over the top and tighten the top screw while pulling taut.

Materials needed
- ★ Your finished cross stitch
- ★ Embroidery hoop
- ★ Scissors
- ★ Needle
- ★ Thread
- ★ Pen/pencil
- ★ Optional: Felt for backing, paint, embellishments

3 Trim away any excess fabric about an inch (2.5cm) from the edge of the hoop.

4 Prepare your thread with a knot – I like to use all six strands – and stitch in a circle using a running stitch. After you make it all the way around, pull to tighten, then secure with a knot. You can use a complementary thread color, or one that blends in. For visibility I used Blanc (white) but would usually choose DMC 310 (black) … obviously.

5 Prepare another needle and thread. Place your felt over the back and join to the fabric using blanket stitch.

How to do a blanket stitch

Cut a length of floss at least three times the circumference of your hoop. Use the full six strands of the skein.

1 Tie a knot in the tail end. Bring your needle up from the back of the felt about a ¼in (0.5cm) from the edge. Loop around the fabric and come up through the same spot at the back of the felt. Each time you go through the felt, pass your needle through your cross stitch fabric to sew them together. This makes your starting stitch and anchors your thread.

2 Start your first blanket stitch. This time going from the front of your felt go down ¼in (0.5cm) to the left or right of your anchor stitch and a ¼in (0.5cm) from the edge of the felt. Make sure your needle is on top of the thread and going through the loop as shown.

3 Continue all the way around your hoop.

4 To finish, connect your last stitch to your first stitch by sliding the needle underneath the loop of your first stitch. Loop through again but, before pulling tight, put your needle through the loop to make a knot. Tighten and then run your floss behind and out of the front of your felt. Pull the thread and snip so that the ends disappear behind the felt.

1 2 3

Don't fret if you run out of thread. Simply tie off and start with a fresh length.
When you have made it all the way around, tie a small knot and then run your floss behind and out of the felt. Pull the thread a bit and snip, and the ends will disappear into your fabric.
You can leave your piece as is in the hoop or add some flair. I have trouble leaving things alone and added black lace and a satin bow, sewn in place with DMC 310 and running stitches.

FINISHING TIPS AND TRICKS

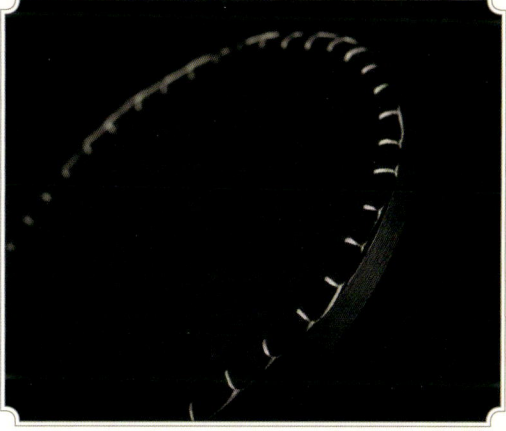

How to frame in a standard picture frame

Framing your stitchcraft can feel a bit daunting, but with the right supplies it is very easy to get it flat and straight in your frame. The best option for mounting board is anything acid-free; sticky board is my preferred choice, but I do use cardboard in a pinch, which is pretty taboo for finishing – cardboard is not acid-free and can degrade your fabric over time, but we are talking decades, not weeks. Acid-free board or mounting board costs more, and I am a bit of a thrifty witch and love to reuse items, especially for smaller, personal stitches. For this finish I used a scrap piece of cardboard from another crafty endeavor. I am willing to take the risk! If you are looking for longevity, definitely use acid-free board.

The method we are covering is called the 'lacing technique'.

Materials needed

★ Your finished stitch
★ Picture frame
★ Sturdy acid-free mounting board (or cardboard)
★ Sewing clips
★ Scissors
★ Ruler
★ Needle
★ Thread (full skein)

FINISHING TIPS AND TRICKS

1 Trim your fabric, leaving about ¾–1in (1.9–2.5cm) outside the edges of your mounting board. I trim the corners off to make them less bulky – just don't trim them too closely!

OPTIONAL STEP: I often like my framed piece to have a bit of a puffed appearance, and so I forego the glass. To achieve this, I put a few layers of felt or fusible foam between the board and the fabric, which results in a neat, pillow-like effect. This method was used on Nevermore, Creepy Carnival, Vintage Ferris Wheel and Valloween Candy Hearts.

2 Center your stitch on the board and clip in place, ensuring it is flat and straight. Alternatively, you can use pins to hold it in place, but I feel the clips work much better. My stitch never budges.

3 Using the full six strands of thread, tie a knot and begin to 'lace' back and forth until your stitch is secure. You don't need to pull very tight; just maintain a consistent medium tension. Place your stitches inside the fabric edge to prevent tearing. It is best to keep the clips on while you are doing this, so that nothing slips. Fold and tuck the corners and give those a lace stitch too.

Don't fret if you run out of thread. Simply tie off and start with a fresh length.

Another option is to use acid-free double-sided tape instead of thread.

Pop the board in your frame and display it so that every person who comes to your haunted home gazes upon its splendor. You did it!

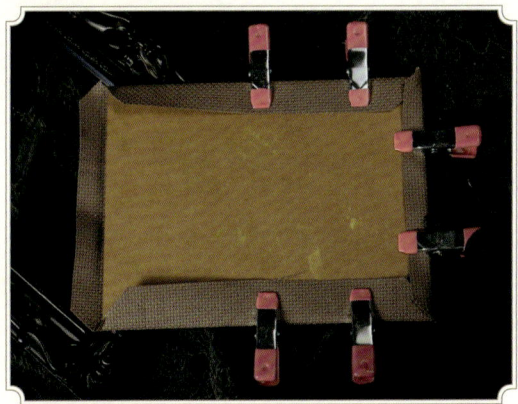

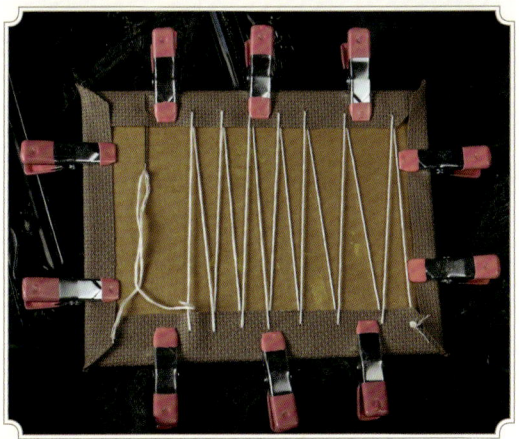

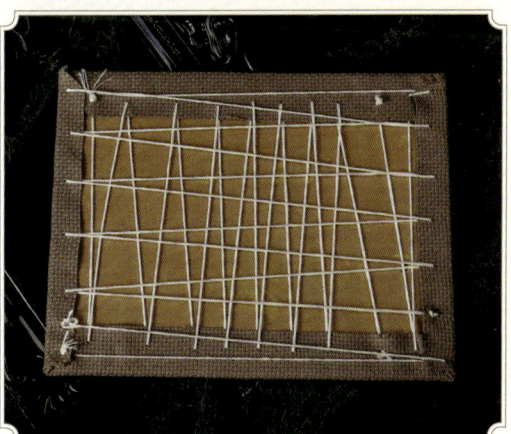

Superstitious stitches cheat sheet

666: seen as a bad omen in many cultures; can also represent the saying 'bad luck comes in threes'.

BIRD: birds also feature in multiple superstitions, the most common being that if a bird flies into a house, it brings an important message. However, if the bird dies, or is white, this symbolizes death.

BLACK CATS: if one crosses your path, it can mean can be good or bad luck, depending on the cultural origins. They were revered in Ancient Egypt and feared in medieval Europe. The fear came from the belief that witches could transform into black cats.

BROKEN MIRROR: breaking a mirror brings bad luck for seven years.

COIN: find a penny, pick it up, all day you'll have good luck! Some believe that heads up means good luck, and tails up means bad luck.

CRACKS: step on a crack and break your mother's back! Derived from the belief that natural cracks in the earth were portals to supernatural realms.

EYES: the left eye twitching means something bad is going to happen, while the right eye twitching means something good will happen.

FOUR-LEAF CLOVER: finding one brings good luck. The leaves of a four-leaf clover represent hope, faith, love and good luck.

HORSESHOE: hanging a horseshoe heels up collects good luck, but if the heels point down, the good luck will fall out. Some believe that heels down will allow good luck to fall on any who passes beneath.

ITCHY HANDS: right hand – money coming in; left hand – money going out.

KNIFE: there are multiple superstitions concerning knives, from ways of giving and receiving them to dropping them. Some are good omens, others aren't.

LADDER: don't walk under one! A ladder, leaning against a wall or standing alone, forms a triangle with the ground, and if you step through it and break it, evil may befall you. The triangle is a sacred symbol for many cultures, and represents a holy trinity.

RABBIT'S FOOT: carrying one brings good luck; losing one brings bad luck.

SALT: if you spill salt, throw some over your shoulder. Salt is a valued weapon in the battle against evil spirits, thanks to its purification and warding capabilities. Tossing it over your left shoulder with your right hand creates a magical barrier that will keep you safe from harm.

SPIDER: as scream-inducing as they are to some, spiders have long been associated with money and good fortune. Their webs also hold meaning: a web over your door means you should expect a visitor, and walking into a web means you may soon see a friend.

THE NUMBER 13: depending on the frame of reference or geographical location, it could mean good or bad luck. Buildings in western countries often leave out the 13th floor, and Friday 13th is considered unlucky. Triskaidekaphobia is the extreme fear of the number 13.

UMBRELLA: opening indoors brings bad luck. If you drop an umbrella, do not pick it up. Instead, have someone else do it for you, or you will have bad luck.

WISHBONE: snapped apart by two people while each makes a wish; the one holding the longer piece is said to have good fortune or a wish granted. If the bone cracks evenly in half, both will have their wishes granted.

Acknowledgments

Thank you to my beautiful mother, Margaret, for her endless support and encouragement. You really shaped who I am today, and I am eternally grateful for you.

Thank you to my spawn, Eli. You always bring a smile to my face. Thank you for always being willing to help me or just talk with random floor sits.

Thank you to my best friend, Rosy, for being a voice of reason, the best video game buddy ever, and for all the laughs and love. Love you, Bat!

Thank you to Sage of Night Spirit Studio, my ethereal 9,000-year-old vampire. My love for you goes beyond your historic birth.

Thank you to my amazing customers. You made all this possible. I still pinch myself to check that all this is real. There is no Witchy Stitcher without you.

A special thank you also to Celia, George, Sian (The Urban Stitches), Rachel (The Gloomy Gremlin), Angela (Sturdy Nerdy Stitchery), Steph (Fine Frog Stitches), Amanda (Bad Stitch), Lindsay (Tusk and Cardinal), Aeon, Kaye, Kelsey and Jen – my fangtastic family, delicious designer pals and marvelous moderators!

Thank you to Bloomsbury for taking a chance on a weird little witch designer, especially Natasha for her guidance, encouragement and expertise, and Austin for the book design.

Thank you to my model stitchers: Lady Gray Stitchcraft, Amber (Dahlia Crypt), Angela Pearson and Paige Reynolds.

Thank you to Alex Black for his support and encouragement throughout the writing process, and for the pattern-themed ghost characters.

A special thank you to my late father, Lawrence. I miss you dearly. The dream finally came true, Dad … I wrote a book!

References

Poe, Edgar Allan, *Ligeia*, The American Museum, Baltimore, 1838
Poe, Edgar Allan, 'The Raven' in *The Raven and Other Poems*, Wiley & Putnam, New York, 1845
Stoker, Bram, *Dracula*, Archibald Constable and Company, London, 1897

Suppliers

Below you will find the suppliers of hand-dyed fabric used in this grimoire, as well as shops that carry all of the basics and necessities. I have separated each shop by country, but many of them offer worldwide shipping. Each of the sources listed below are ones that I personally use, have worked closely with, or have come highly recommended by international members of the cross stitch coven.

Canada

GENERAL SUPPLIES AND ORIGINAL PATTERNS AND ACCESSORIES

The Witchy Stitcher (Calgary, Alberta)
thewitchystitcher.com

GENERAL SUPPLIES

Michaels (multiple locations)
canada.michaels.com
Stitch It Central (London, Ontario)
stitchitcentral.ca
Traditional Stitches (Calgary, Alberta)
traditionalstitches.com

ORIGINAL FABRIC AND THREAD

Hand Dyed by Rolanda (online)
etsy.com/ca/shop/HandDyedbyRolanda

United States

GENERAL SUPPLIES

123 Stitch (Lewisville, Texas)
123stitch.com *the most popular choice for North America*
Everything Cross Stitch (online)
everythingcrossstitch.com
Joann Fabrics (multiple locations)
joann.com
Michaels (multiple locations)
michaels.com
Starlight Stitchery (online)
starlightstitch.com

GENERAL SUPPLIES AND ORIGINAL FABRIC AND THREAD

BeStitchMe (Moline, Illinois)
bestitchme.com
Colour and Cotton Needleworks (Manchester, Missouri)
colourandcotton.com
Mystic Fabrics (online)
mysticfabrics.com
Under The Sea Fabrics (San Antonio, Texas)
undertheseafabrics.com
Witch's Garden Crafts (online)
etsy.com/shop/Witchsgardencrafts

PROJECT KEEPERS AND GRIME GUARDS

The Golden Familiars (online)
thegoldenfamiliars.com

SUPPLIERS AND STITCHING CREDITS

Australia
GENERAL SUPPLIES

JK's Cross Stitch Supplies (online)
jkscrossstitchsupplies.com.au

GENERAL SUPPLIES, SPECIAL COLLABORATIONS AND ORIGINAL THREAD

Cottage Garden Threads (online)
cottagegardenthreads.com.au

ORIGINAL FABRIC AND PATTERNS

Fox and Rabbit Designs (online)
foxandrabbit.com

Hungary
ORIGINAL FABRIC

xJuDesign (online)
etsy.com/shop/xJuDesign

Italy
ORIGINAL ACCESSORIES, FABRIC AND PATTERNS

The Primitive Hare (online)
theprimitivehare.shop

United Kingdom
GENERAL CROSS STITCH SUPPLIES

Hobbycraft (multiple locations)
hobbycraft.co.uk
Lakeside Needlecraft (online)
lakesideneedlecraft.co.uk
Lovecrafts (online)
lovecrafts.com

ORIGINAL AND BESPOKE FABRIC

The Stitchy Ferret (online)
thestitchyferret.com

Stitching credits

All stitched and finished (and framed, where applicable) by Meg Black (The Witchy Stitcher), unless stated below.

Bat Coven
Stitched by: Lady Gray Stitchcraft

Three of Besoms
Stitched by: Lady Gray Stitchcraft

Witch's Cauldron
Stitched by: Lady Gray Stitchcraft

Memento Mori
Stitched by: Paige Reynolds

Victorian Haunt
Stitched by: Amber (Dahlia Crypt)

Nevermore
Stitched by: Angela Pearson

Dracula's Castle
Stitched by: Lady Gray Stitchcraft

Carnivorous Plants
Stitched by: Paige Reynolds

Vintage Halloween Dolls
Stitched by: Paige Reynolds

Creepy Carnival
Stitched by: Lady Gray Stitchcraft

Happy Owl-O-Ween
Stitched by: Paige Reynolds

Haunting Hour
Stitched by: Paige Reynolds

GingerDead House
Stitched by: Paige Reynolds

Valloween Hearts
Stitched by: Paige Reynolds